Collaborative Units that Work

Collaborative Units that Work

TEAMS Award Winners

Kate Vande Brake, Editor

LINWORTH BOOKS

LIBRARIES UNLIMITED
An Imprint of ABC-CLIO, LLC

Santa Barbara, California • Denver, Colorado • Oxford, England

Copyright 2010 by Libraries Unlimited

All rights reserved. No part of this publication may be reproduced,
stored in a retrieval system, or transmitted, in any form or by any means,
electronic, mechanical, photocopying, recording, or otherwise, except for
the inclusion of brief quotations in a review, without prior permission
in writing from the publisher.

Library of Congress Cataloging-in-Publication Data

Collaborative units that work : teams award winners / edited by Kate Vande Brake.
   p. cm.
"A Linworth Publishing book."
Includes bibliographical references and index.
ISBN-13: 978-1-58683-349-7 (pbk. : alk. paper)
ISBN-10: 1-58683-349-9 (pbk. : alk. paper) 1. Teaching teams. 2. School librarian participation in curriculum planning. I. Vande Brake, Kate.
   LB1029.T4C655 2010
   371.14'8—dc22   2009021197

14 13 12 11 10   1 2 3 4 5

This book is also available on the World Wide Web as an eBook.
Visit www.abc-clio.com for details.

ABC-CLIO, LLC
130 Cremona Drive, P.O. Box 1911
Santa Barbara, California 93116-1911

This book is printed on acid-free paper ∞
Manufactured in the United States of America

Copyright Acknowledgments

The editor and publisher gratefully acknowledge permission for use of the following material:

Standards for the 21st Century Learner are excerpted from Standards for the 21st-Century Learner by the American Association of School Librarians, a division of the American Library Association, copyright © 2007 American Library Association. Available for download at www.ala.org/aasl/standards. Reprinted with permission.

National Education Technology Standards for Students, 2007 from NETS for Students: National Educational Technology Standards for Students, Second Edition, © 2007, ISTE® (International Society for Technology in Education), www.iste.org. All rights reserved.

Standards for the English Language Arts, by the International Reading Association and the National Council of Teachers of English, Copyright 1996 by the International Reading Association and the National Council of Teachers of English. Reprinted with permission. http://www.ncte.org/standards.

Rather than put a trademark symbol with every occurrence of a trademarked name, we state that we are using the names only in an editorial fashion and to the benefit of the trademark owner, with no intention of infringement of the trademark.

Contents

Figures ix
Acknowledgments xi
Introduction xiii
National Standards and the Collaborative Units xvii

SECTION I: ELEMENTARY COLLABORATION UNITS

CHAPTER 1: Authors' Night 3
Betsey Kennedy and Barbara Powell-Schager
Big Shanty Elementary School, Georgia

  Project Overview. 3
  Timeline 6
  Roles Defined 6
  Measuring Success 7
  Funding Your Project. 8
  Materials and Resources 9
  Sustaining This Project 9

CHAPTER 2: The Global Schoolhouse Project. 11
Cally Flickinger and Jennifer Opel
Chamberlin School, Vermont

  Project Overview. 11
  Timeline 13
  Roles Defined 13
  Measuring Success 14
  Funding Your Project. 15
  Materials and Resources 16
  Sustaining This Project 16

CHAPTER 3: Take-Home DVD: Improving Emergent Literacy Skills. 17
T. K. Cassidy and Betsy Thornton
Dug Gap Elementary School, Georgia

  Project Overview. 17
  Timeline 19
  Roles Defined 19
  Measuring Success 20
  Funding Your Project. 21
  Materials and Resources 21
  Sustaining This Project 22

CHAPTER 4: Thinking Like a Scientist 23
Mary Karlovec and Anne Michael
Windsor Elementary School, Ohio

Project Overview. 23
Timeline 24
Roles Defined 25
Measuring Success 25
Funding Your Project. 26
Materials and Resources 27
Sustaining This Project 27

SECTION II: MIDDLE SCHOOL COLLABORATION UNITS

CHAPTER 5: Where in the World Are Our Middle School Students Now? 31
Barbara Adair, Rick Norman, John Scrivano, and Dana Thompson
New Smyrna Beach Middle School, Florida

Project Overview. 31
Timeline 33
Roles Defined 33
Measuring Success 34
Funding Your Project. 35
Materials and Resources 35
Sustaining This Project 36

CHAPTER 6: Mathematical Nightmares 37
Nelle Cox, Shari Galgano, and JoAnn Reynolds
Dover Air Base Middle School, Delaware

Project Overview. 37
Timeline 41
Roles Defined 41
Measuring Success 43
Funding Your Project. 46
Materials and Resources 46
Sustaining This Project 46

CHAPTER 7: One Book, One School 49
Chris Altobello, David Guest, Kendra Hamby, John McCollum, Debbie Pace,
Sharon Scott, Brooks Spencer, LaDonna Walker, and Susan Wilson
Osceola Middle School, Florida

Project Overview. 49
Timeline 52
Roles Defined 52
Measuring Success 55
Funding Your Project. 59

Materials and Resources 60
Sustaining This Project 60

SECTION III: HIGH SCHOOL COLLABORATION UNITS

CHAPTER 8: Teen Expressions 63
Lorraine Grochowski and Corrine Richardson
Booker T. Washington Senior High School, Florida

Project Overview 63
Timeline 65
Roles Defined 66
Measuring Success 66
Funding Your Project 68
Materials and Resources 69
Sustaining This Project 69

CHAPTER 9: Comic Relief: Using Graphic Novels with ESL Students 71
Leila "Bee" Manship and Chasity Markle
Concord High School, North Carolina

Project Overview 71
Timeline 73
Roles Defined 73
Measuring Success 74
Funding Your Project 76
Materials and Resources 76
Sustaining This Project 77

CHAPTER 10: Internet Safety 79
Billie Esser and Mary Anne Knowles
Jefferson West High School, Kansas

Project Overview 79
Timeline 80
Roles Defined 81
Measuring Success 81
Funding Your Project 82
Materials and Resources 82
Sustaining This Project 83

CHAPTER 11: Advanced Academic Literacies 85
Michaelyn Hein, Martha Hickson, Mary Loder, Caitlin Ryan, and Lauren Sheldon
North Hunterdon High School, New Jersey

Project Overview 85
Timeline 88
Roles Defined 88

Measuring Success 89
Funding Your Project... 90
Materials and Resources 90
Sustaining This Project 91

CHAPTER 12: Culinary Reading Program 93
Wilhelmina DeNunzio and Carol Faas
Eastside High School, Florida

Project Overview.. 93
Timeline 95
Roles Defined 95
Measuring Success 96
Funding Your Project... 97
Materials and Resources 97
Sustaining This Project 98

Works Cited 101
Index 103

Figures

FIGURE S.1: Standards for the 21st-Century Learner xvii
FIGURE S.2: National Education Technology Standards for Students 2007 xviii
FIGURE S.3: NCTE/IRA Standards for the English Language Arts xix
FIGURE 3.1: Kindergarten Readiness Assessment. 20
FIGURE 4.1: Student Test Results and Grade Two Science Indicators 26
FIGURE 6.1: Example of Web Page Rubric 39
FIGURE 6.2: Example of Parent Permission Letter 42
FIGURE 6.3: State Assessment Results 43
FIGURE 6.4: Example of Knowledge Survey 45
FIGURE 7.1: Example of a Reference Scavenger Hunt 53
FIGURE 7.2: Example of an Interactive Test 56
FIGURE 7.3: Example of a Writing Challenge. 57
FIGURE 8.1: Impact of *Teen Expressions* on Fourth-Quarter Student Grades. 68
FIGURE 9.1: Circulation of Graphic Novels 76
FIGURE 10.1: Internet Safety Information Online. 82
FIGURE 11.1: Example of a One-Minute Survey 87
FIGURE 11.2: Self-Assessment of *Advanced Academic Literacies* Participants. 90
FIGURE 12.1: Resource List for *Culinary Reading Program* 98

Acknowledgments

I would like to thank Cyndee Anderson for her leadership and guidance. Her professionalism and wonderful spirit are inspiring. Thank you to my husband, Mike, for selflessly giving of his time so that I could work on this project. His consistent help and support are far underappreciated, but I can do very little without him. Also, thank you to my son, Harry, who gives me every reason to do my best as an example for the man I hope he will become.

Introduction

Do you dream of a unit or course in which your students meet or exeed your district's standards without realizing how much they have learned? Are you ready to try something new and willing to work with peers at your school? This book is designed to give collaborative teaching teams fresh ideas and real application, taking the guesswork out of designing a creative, standards-based project from which all of your students can benefit.

In the pages that follow, you will find the winning units of the Thomson/Gale Library Media Connections TEAMS Award. The Thomson/Gale Media Connections TEAMS Award, started in 2007, recognizes and encourages the critical effort of collaboration between the teacher and the media specialist to promote student learning and increase student achievement.

A panel of education and school library professionals evaluated these award-winning units based on a demonstrated collaboration between media specialists and teacher, effective techniques that positively impact student learning and achievement, support received from school leadership, and the ability for others to replicate this project. The units represent some of the best practices in which school librarians and teachers are engaged today.

Winners wrote articles for Library Media Connection that explained their collaborative units and shared some of the excitement that surrounded the success of these projects. To learn more about the TEAMS Award, go to <www.galeschools.com/TEAMS/>.

Why Collaborate?

While collaboration between media specialists and teachers is second nature to some, it is uncharted territory—and a little scary—for others. Education experts agree that collaboration is a critical step for developing strong curriculum that launches students to success on standardized tests. Keith Curry Lance and his associates, in *How School Librarians Help Kids Achieve Standards: The Second Colorado Study,* found as a result of their studies "the importance of a collaborative approach to information literacy. Test scores rise in both elementary and middle schools as library media specialists and teachers work together" (3).

Projects included in this book are data-driven and evidence-based, key components for measuring student success as well as earning necessary support from the school and administration. Michael Eisenberg, widely known as the co-creator of The Big6, says it is important today that the library media specialist collaborate with peers to create units that positively impact student performance on standardized tests.

> I recognize that one lesson here and there will not have much of an impact on student performance. However, over time, repeated lessons that focus on the same information skills—targeted to questions in the same format and style that appear on statewide tests, taught collaboratively by the teacher-librarian and classroom teacher—can make a difference. (29)

Ross J. Todd, director of the Center for International Scholarship in School Libraries, is a leading researcher whose studies focus on the role of the school library in the 21st century and school reform. He goes further to say that evidence-based practice can actually enhance the impact of the library media program within the school. "By emphasizing outcomes, EBP [evidence-based practice] shifts the focus from articulating what school librarians do to what students achieve. Accordingly, EBP validates that quality learning outcomes can be achieved through the school library and that the school librarian is an important instructional partner" (par. 17).

How Can I Use This Book?

Every state has a set of educational standards for its students, and every school district has a unique method it uses to meet those standards. While this book does not define how each project can fulfill the requirements of your particular state, it does identify standards from the:

- International Reading Association
- National Council of Teachers of English
- American Association of School Librarians, and
- International Society for Technology in Education.

Also note that some projects fulfill additional standards in other curricular areas. Web sites are available to help you navigate the standards and benchmarks for K-12 education, such as McREL: Mid-Continent Research for Education and Learning <www.mcrel.org/standards-benchmarks/>. The national standards are listed after the Introduction.

The units are presented in a format that summarizes each project and details some of the requirements you will need to replicate the project in your school. A section called "Roles Defined" identifies various responsibilities of the media specialist and the collaborating teacher.

"Measuring Success" offers questions you might ask and suggests objective ways to evaluate the success of the project at your school. This section shows you how evidence-based practices in addition to anecdotal and participatory evidence can prove the success of the program.

A section for "Funding" is included, as is a section outlining "Materials and Resources" you will need for the project or unit. Use this as a starting point for finding the resources you will need to make the project a reality at your school.

> **TIP**
>
> Grant writing is an important skill to have. Foundations, corporations, and government entities often have thousands of dollars to donate to educational projects, but it's up to you to apply. *Write Grants, Get Money* (Linworth Publishing, 2008), by Cynthia Anderson and Kathi Knop, is a great resource for those interested in perfecting their grant-writing skills.

"Sustaining This Project" offers suggestions on how to incorporate the collaborative project into your school's long-term plans. These additional ideas may give you realistic options for developing a project into something your school could use today.

Within each unit are examples and suggestions from the unit's authors that may help you brainstorm ways you can incorporate the project in your school. From tips to building community support to specific ideas for activities, these pull-out boxes provide examples to help you move forward with your own project.

The contact information included with each unit is there for a reason, as well. The authors of these units are excited to share with you their ideas and suggestions for improvement upon them. Learn from those who have already put the program in place. Consider contacting them with your questions.

Are You Ready?

One reason library media specialists are unique is that they must make themselves knowledgeable in every subject area to be able to meet the literacy needs of each student at every grade level. Another reason for their uniqueness is that they also see a big picture of their school and

> **Ultimately, data-driven collaboration succeeds in meeting standards set by your district and renews an excitement for learning—for both students and teachers.**

often are heavily invested in the success of the students they see each week.

Sometimes, even the most motivated library media specialist can hear the word "collaboration" and immediately think of a number of challenges she will face if she embarks on such a project.

The projects presented here represent best practices that are occurring all across the country, and they provide a plan for integrating these practices in your own school. The educators who collaborated on these projects are giving you the secrets to their success in the hopes that you, too, will find fresh, innovative ways to motivate students and peers.

Author and media specialist Toni Buzzeo has compiled several books focusing on the subject of collaboration. Her interviews with media specialists and other educational professionals offer proof of the extraordinary educational benefit of teacher/teacher-librarian collaboration. "Through collaboration, information skills are taught in context of new and creative units of study. As a result, students benefit and achievement rises" (Buzzeo 33).

Ultimately, data-driven collaboration succeeds in meeting standards set by your district and renews an excitement for learning—for both students and teachers.

National Standards and the Collaborative Units

Standards for the 21st Century Learner

Learners use skills, resources, & tools to:

1. Inquire, think critically, and gain knowledge

2. Draw conclusions, make informed decisions, apply knowledge to new situations, and create new knowledge.

3. Share knowledge and participate ethically and productively as members of our democratic society.

4. Pursue personal and aesthetic growth.

Excerpted from Standards for the 21st-Century Learner by the American Association of School Librarians, a division of the American Library Association, copyright © 2007 American Library Association. Available for download at www.ala.org/aasl/standards. Reprinted with permission.

Figure S.1: Standards for the 21st-Century Learner

National Educational Technology Standards for Students

Creativity and Innovation

Communication and Collaboration

Research and Information Fluency

Critical Thinking, Problem Solving, and Decision Making

Digital Citizenship

Technology Operations and Concepts

NETS for Students: National Educational Technology Standards for Students, Second Edition, © 2007, ISTE® (International Society for Technology in Education), www.iste.org. All rights reserved.

Figure S.2: National Educational Technology Standards for Students 2007

NCTE/IRA Standards for the English Language Arts

	1. Students read a wide range of print and non-print texts to build an understanding of texts, of themselves, and of the cultures of the United States and the world; to acquire new information; to respond to the needs and demands of society and the workplace; and for personal fulfillment. Among these texts are fiction and nonfiction, classic and contemporary works.
	2. Students read a wide range of literature from many periods in many genres to build an understanding of the many dimensions (e.g., philosophical, ethical, aesthetic) of human experience.
	3. Students apply a wide range of strategies to comprehend, interpret, evaluate, and appreciate texts. They draw on their prior experience, their interactions with other readers and writers, their knowledge of word meaning and of other texts, their word identification strategies, and their understanding of textual features (e.g., sound-letter correspondence, sentence structure, context, graphics).
	4. Students adjust their use of spoken, written, and visual language (e.g., conventions, style, vocabulary) to communicate effectively with a variety of audiences and for different purposes.
	5. Students employ a wide range of strategies as they write and use different writing process elements appropriately to communicate with different audiences for a variety of purposes.
	6. Students apply knowledge of language structure, language conventions (e.g., spelling and punctuation), media techniques, figurative language, and genre to create, critique, and discuss print and non-print texts.
	7. Students conduct research on issues and interests by generating ideas and questions, and by posing problems. They gather, evaluate, and synthesize data from a variety of sources (e.g., print and non-print texts, artifacts, people) to communicate their discoveries in ways that suit their purpose and audience.
	8. Students use a variety of technological and information resources (e.g., libraries, databases, computer networks, video) to gather and synthesize information and to create and communicate knowledge.
	9. Students develop an understanding of and respect for diversity in language use, patterns, and dialects across cultures, ethnic groups, geographic regions, and social roles.
	10. Students whose first language is not English make use of their first language to develop competency in the English language arts and to develop understanding of content across the curriculum.
	11. Students participate as knowledgeable, reflective, creative, and critical members of a variety of literacy communities.
	12. Students use spoken, written, and visual language to accomplish their own purposes (e.g., for learning, enjoyment, persuasion, and the exchange of information).

Standards for the English Language Arts, by the International Reading Association and the National Council of Teachers of English, Copyright 1996 by the International Reading Association and the National Council of Teachers of English. Reprinted with permission.

Figure S.3: NCTE/IRA Standards for the English Language Arts

SECTION I

Elementary Collaboration Units

CHAPTER 1

Authors' Night

Betsey Kennedy, Fifth-Grade Teacher
Barbara Powell-Schager, Library Media Specialist

Big Shanty Elementary School

1575 Ben King Road
Kennesaw, Georgia 30144
(678) 594-8023
www.cobbk12.org/BigShanty/

Project Overview

The school improvement plan at this Georgia elementary school placed special emphasis on the improvement of student writing as well as the development of teachers' understanding of the writing process. The national focus on testing-required areas drew the focus away from local initiatives like improving writing skills, and, more broadly, encouraging a love for writing.

Big Shanty Elementary fifth-grade teacher Betsey Kennedy and library media specialist Barbara Powell-Schager set out to bring to focus back to writing. Recognizing that writing is a key element of state standards across the country, they set a goal of revitalizing interest in the writing process, and this led to a series of activities, events, and contests, all of which focused on making writing a part of the everyday life at the school. When they saw their school becoming a community of writers, they began planning for *Authors' Night* to celebrate the students' accomplishments.

After initial planning, Kennedy and Powell-Schager started the school year by organizing weekly readings of published poetry by third- and fifth-grade students on the school's weekly televised newscast. The positive response led to a monthly poetry contest in which students could enter original poems for a chance to be published in the school newsletter and broadcast to the school through televised announcements. Student interest climbed with each contest, and writing quality improved.

This was only the beginning.

> **TIP**
>
> To encourage greater participation, highlight interesting writing projects during staff training sessions and allow more students to share their writing on your school's weekly news broadcasts, in the school newsletter, and in the school writing anthology.

During a February staff meeting, the team presented the idea for a school-wide *Authors' Night*. The evening was to be a celebration of student compositions, but it required participation and support from throughout the school if it was to be a success. They provided teachers with a list of possible presentation ideas and even worked with a local restaurant to award a gift certificate to the teacher with the most students in attendance. In many cases, teachers selected projects for their class presentations that corresponded with lessons already in progress. Others saw the event as an opportunity to work on larger, integrated projects that involved writing and other content areas, such as creating video presentations about silent movies of the 1920s.

Advertising the event both within the school and in the community was critical. To begin, the teachers arranged for an author visit. Then, Kennedy and Powell-Schager worked with students to write and produce video commercials advertising the event on the school's televised morning announcements. They distributed flyers to every class and to students at Big Shanty's feeder school. The team invited county supervisors and officials and printed a student-designed bookmark to advertise the event. Finally, the two became walking billboards, wearing t-shirts designed by Kennedy and fish-shaped hats publicizing and generating interest in the upcoming event.

Twelve classrooms participated in *Authors' Night*. Powell-Schager, who had experience with similar events, created a schedule for the evening that allowed students and the community to see and visit several presentations. She also arranged for a pizza dinner to accommodate working parents.

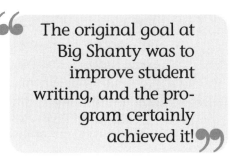

"The original goal at Big Shanty was to improve student writing, and the program certainly achieved it!"

Meanwhile, students showcased their talent at the Bohemian Poetry Café, where students recited their poetry while the audience sipped hot chocolate and around a campfire, where they told cowboy tales. One third-grade class used a Microsoft PowerPoint presentation to display its compositions about going to the zoo, while a fourth-grade class shared "Star Stories: Constellation Formation."

TIP

Find a local story teller to present to students. Work with your parents' organization to fund the presentation.

The original goal at Big Shanty was to improve student writing, and the program certainly achieved it! Of 65 elementary schools in the school district, Big Shanty was ranked No. 15 in the number of students meeting or exceeding standards on the Georgia fifth-grade writing assessment. The students' average score on that exam was higher than the county and state averages for fifth grade. That was significant data to support the positive impact that collaborative focus can make on student learning.

Teachers, students, parents, and county-level supervisors inundated Kennedy and Powell-Schager with requests to make *Authors' Night* an annual event. The first year, 174 students participated, and there is interest in doubling the number for subsequent events.

GETTING SUPPORT

Invite school district leaders, local elected officials, and community members to your event. Provide food with the help of local businesses to cater to working parents.

Timeline

Planning for *Authors' Night* began in September with the culminating event, *Authors' Night*, in April. The collaborating teachers held regular planning, status-report, and problem-solving meetings throughout the year and included other participating faculty when appropriate. They also organized monthly poetry contest and quarterly writing fairs for students to submit original work in a variety of writing genres.

Roles Defined

The Library Media Specialist Is Responsible For:

- Judging entries in the school poetry contests and writing fair.
- Introducing *Authors' Night* to colleagues at regular staff meeting.
- Organizing a visit by a storyteller/author and preparing the author's schedule, securing funding, and managing book sales.
- Coordinating and producing the school's televised morning announcements to highlight the writing initiatives, including student poetry readings and advertisements related to *Authors' Night*.
- Printing and distributing flyers advertising *Authors' Night* to students.
- Creating a schedule for *Authors' Night*.
- Working with educational partners to provide dinner at event.
- Trouble-shooting and serving as the point-person at *Authors' Night*.

The Teacher(s) Is Responsible For:

- Organizing monthly poetry contests and submitting winning entries to be published in the school newsletter.
- Introducing *Authors' Night* to colleagues at regular staff meeting.
- Planning the school writing fair: organizing entries, coordinating judges, finalizing scores.
- Creating flyers and bookmarks to advertise *Authors' Night*.
- Helping students write and practice advertisements for *Authors' Night* to be televised as part of the school announcements.
- Preparing a handout for attendees detailing the schedule of events for *Authors' Night*.
- Working with class to prepare presentation for *Authors' Night*.
- Acting as liaison for and providing a list of presentation ideas to staff members who choose to participate *in Authors' Night*.

> **TIP**
> To make sure all of your students will have an opportunity to present and view their peers, schedule concurrent sessions. Allow attendees to map out which four sessions they would like to visit, and provide a systematic way of changing sessions.

- Developing a soft-cover literary anthology of student work featuring winners from poetry contests, winning entries and honorable mentions from the writing fair, and illustrations from volunteer classes. Working with local publishing company to bind the anthology and sell to students at reduced cost.
- Applying for grant funding.

Measuring Success

Anecdotal evidence: How do teachers respond? Do students incorporate the new terminology related to the various writing genres? Are parents pleased with their child's writing development? At Big Shanty, Kennedy and Powell-Schager were pleasantly rewarded by seeing visible pride in each of their students who participated in *Authors' Night*. Other students who attended the evening were eager and willing to try the new writing techniques they listened to at *Authors' Night*. Teachers told the organizers of students who introduced themselves as "talented writers" and others who set for themselves the goal of being published in the school's writing anthology.

Testing evidence: Has the school experienced an increase in the average testing scores in writing after students have participated in several months of preparation for Authors' Night? Yes, it has. Big Shanty Assistant Principal Patrick O'Connell attributed the testing success to *Authors' Night*. In his review of the program and the events leading to it, he told the teachers, "I have zero doubt that the enthusiasm generated from school-wide writing projects, such as *Authors' Night*, contributed to Big Shanty's great success on the Grade 5 Writing Test." Of the 65 district elementary schools, Big Shanty was ranked No. 15 in the number of students meeting or exceeding standards on the Georgia fifth-grade writing assessment. The students' average score on that exam was higher than the county and state averages for fifth grade.

> **Big Shanty Assistant Principal Patrick O'Connell attributed the testing success to *Authors' Night*. In his review of the program and the events leading to it, he told the teachers, "I have zero doubt that the enthusiasm generated from school-wide writing projects, such as *Authors' Night*, contributed to Big Shanty's great success on the Grade 5 Writing Test."**

Participatory evidence: Are students encouraged to submit essays to local and national contests? Does the rate of participation in writing contests increase in comparison to the rate years past? The year before beginning this project, only 62 students entered the school writing fair. The number ballooned to 140 entries the year this project was instituted. The quality of the entries improved, and Big Shanty claimed the top two places at the district's fifth-grade writing competition.

Funding Your Project

Look for local support. At Big Shanty Elementary, the library media specialist organized a pizza dinner with the help of a local pizza restaurant that was already a partner in education. The restaurant arranged to deliver pizzas to the school and sell them at a discounted price. The profit from the dinner was used to fund future *Authors' Night* events.

Create a product. The student writing anthology was sold to parents and students and generated enough profit to pay for future publication of student work as well as to purchase professional materials for teachers.

Research grant opportunities. To help pay for the first publication of the student writing anthology, Betsey Kennedy applied for and received a $350 minigrant from the Ezra Jack Keats Foundation <www.ezra-jack-keats.org> to cover start-up costs for the unit. The grants are awarded to schools that are planning unique projects, big or small, that help students connect to reading and writing. Kennedy, who had never applied for a grant previously, said the application process was not difficult and was great training for larger grant applications. When planning the application, she said to think of something new that students would not have experienced before. It is the unique, engaging programs that are most likely to be funded.

> **Betsey Kennedy applied for and received a $350 minigrant from the Ezra Jack Keats Foundation <www.ezra-jack-keats.org> to cover start-up costs for the unit.**

Materials and Resources

- Access to a school-wide broadcasting system for weekly poetry readings and advertisements for *Authors' Night*
- School newsletter, electronic or print, for publishing original writings and publicity related to *Authors' Night*

Sustaining This Project

Authors' Night is a natural fit for schools that are looking for a program to improve student writing skills that can be implemented from year to year. By incorporating recommendations made by teachers, the collaborative team will continue to improve the program from year-to-year. This will also encourage greater participation because of the entire school's involvement.

Publicizing the event throughout the school district will also increase interest in the program and ensure that it becomes an annual effort as opposed to a one-time program. Sustainability of the program for the school is critical to long-term development in student writing and achievement on tests.

Finally, using the same formula of collaboration, creativity, and a focus on standards to create similar events in other curricular areas will additionally benefit students. At Big Shanty, the teachers already planned to begin a family math night in which entire families could interact and provide support for the learning of important math skills. Just picture a school buzzing with young "Counts and Countesses" playing math games, holding math bees, and solving difficult problems with the help of their parents, educators, and community members!

GETTING SUPPORT

Don't be afraid to share your ideas with others in your school district. The collaboration may provide you with additional tips to incorporate your event with others, such as public library events. Remember, any exposure equals publicity for your students and long-term success for your event!

CHAPTER 2

The Global Schoolhouse Project

Cally Flickinger, Library Media Specialist
Jennifer Opel, ELL Teacher

Chamberlin School

262 White Street
South Burlington, Vermont 05403
(802) 652-7400
<http://chamberlin.sbschools.net/>

Project Overview

Meeting the needs of students who represent a wide range of languages and socioeconomic status is challenging for many schools. At Chamberlin School, more than 15 home languages were spoken by the school's 240 students. In fact, 10 percent of these students did not speak English as their primary language. Library media specialist Cally Flickinger and English Language Learner (ELL) teacher Jennifer Opel collaborated to create a data-driven project that promotes awareness of and appreciation for cultural diversity. In the process, the teachers were focused on increasing the critical-thinking skills and information literacy of their students.

The *Global Schoolhouse* project was a research unit for fifth-grade students. Working in groups of four, students were assigned a country to research. The group was responsible for a poster board display or PowerPoint presentation about the country that included its schools and literacy rate, a map, and other information specific to the nation. Each group conducted a videotaped interview of someone who had attended school in that country or someone who had visited that country. The teacher and the media specialist then instructed one member of each group how to edit the video and create a DVD for viewing. The school's art and music teachers also contributed. They taught mini research lessons in the art and music classes to help students find representative art and music for their chosen countries.

> **TIP**
> Utilize other teachers in the school to help in areas where they have expertise.

The unit culminated with an evening event in which students were given a nine-foot by nine-foot area in the school cafeteria to decorate in the manner of a schoolroom in the country they researched. Guests who visited this *Global Schoolhouse* could attend "school," where they would learn what it was like to live in that particular country. At each stop they participated in the following activities:

1. They were each given a passport, and students stamped this passport with a student-created stamp. The stamp reflected something from the culture of that country and was designed with the help of the art teacher.

2. At each "schoolroom," a PowerPoint display ran with the results of the students' research.

3. With the help of families, students prepared and brought authentic food for tasting at the event.

Each of these engaging activities helped to make the journey to these various countries come alive for students, staff, and families.

> **GETTING SUPPORT**
> Invite families to participate by asking them to bring authentic food of their cultures or to gather artifacts for the schoolrooms.

Students learned a variety of research skills and were able to access information from print, Internet, and primary sources. Once students accessed the information they sought, they learned to compile their information into a report format as well as a presentation format. The ability to repackage information and express it compellingly is on target with educator and technology guru David Warlick. In fact, the American Association of School Librarians emphasizes the importance of skills in multiple literacies, including digital, visual, and textual, in its *Standards for the 21st Century Learner* (AASL 3).

> "Not only did the students learn about each other, but the project brought families out to learn about their school's community, as well."

Students also walked away with knowledge of different countries of the world, and they had valuable practice in information literacy skills, including research, teaching and persuading others using technology, and presentation of information. They found confidence not only in the knowledge they were able to glean from their research but also in their abilities to present that information to others.

The day following the community-wide *Global Schoolhouse*, the entire school was invited to experience school in various countries. In a school where the range of cultural diversity could easily have created divisions among its population, the *Global Schoolhouse* project built a bridge. Not only did the students learn about each other, but the project brought families out to learn about their school's community, as well.

Timeline

This project had a long timeline. Teachers began to plan during the summer, identifying personal strengths that would enhance the unit and determining how to balance the responsibilities of the unit with current workloads. The unit began in late October and ended in early February. During this four-month period, students learned and practiced research skills and worked in groups to plan and prepare their presentations for the *Global Schoolhouse*.

Roles Defined

The Library Media Specialist Is Responsible For:

- Working with the teacher to develop a unit that aligned with the educational standards and benchmarks.

- Sharing direct instruction of the students with the teacher.
- Teaching students to use reference materials, such as books, encyclopedias, and Internet sources, and how to compile a bibliography.
- Instructing students to ask good research questions and make inferences based on research.
- Coordinating with any additional teachers at the school whose expertise may enhance the students' final products.

The Teacher(s) Is Responsible For:

- Giving students experience working with nonfiction conventions and recognizing their value in research.
- Assessing weekly student group skills and research skills.
- Creating outline formats for students to follow when collecting and organizing their research.
- Differentiating instruction for any special needs among the students and coordinating with support teachers to ensure that the appropriate educational standards are being fulfilled.

Measuring Success

Anecdotal evidence: How does the school community respond? At Chamberlin School, the parents of the students showed amazing support by offering their knowledge and time. The fathers of two students at the school—neither of whom was in the fifth grade—donated 40 hours of their time to assist in video editing instruction and the creation of 11 DVDs of individual interviews conducted by the students. Another parent said, "I've rarely seen such in-depth presentations on a foreign culture. The displays were authentically detailed without stereotypical imaging."

> **GETTING SUPPORT**
>
> Offer parent training on various technologies used in the project to encourage parents to later become mentors.

Testing evidence: How can you assess student work to show understanding? Using the South Burlington Curriculum Standards for Fifth Grade, the teachers used qualitative and quantitative results to measure success according to these standards. Students completed homework assignments to practice various critical-thinking and research skills they would need to complete the project. The teachers assessed the research, display boards, graphs, maps, and PowerPoint presentations for factual accuracy. The team created a rubric for each student group, and it served as a checklist for the necessary components of each assignment within the project.

> Another parent said, "I've rarely seen such in-depth presentations on a foreign culture. The displays were authentically detailed without stereotypical imaging."

Participatory evidence: How many students remain actively involved during the entire project? How many families attend the final event? Every student who participated in the project created the display boards, dressed in costume, and completed bibliographies of his or her research. Every one of the students who was taught to use the digital video camera and edit the video material did so successfully. Additionally, 95 percent of the families were able to attend the *Global Schoolhouse*, and 80 percent of these families provided food for the event. Research shows that, "When family members commonly engage with teachers or other school staff, students adjust more easily to classroom activities and their teachers at both the elementary and secondary levels, resulting in improved student performance" (SEDL 2).

Funding Your Project

Utilize existing resources. The Chamberlin School media center had the initial resources students needed to complete their research. They used encyclopedias and nonfiction books, as well as Internet databases and teacher-selected general Internet sites specific to the countries of research. The school also pooled its existing resources to provide adequate numbers of televisions and computers for student use.

Include other staff at your school. Although the core collaborating team included the library media

> "When family members commonly engage with teachers or other school staff, students adjust more easily to classroom activities and their teachers at both the elementary and secondary levels, resulting in improved student performance" (SEDL 2).

specialist and the ELL teacher, the collaboration extended to others in the school. The reading teacher, writing consultant, principal, and special educators all played key roles in working with student groups.

Materials and Resources

- Computers and/or laptops for individual student research and for display at the *Global Schoolhouse*
- Nonfiction books on each of the countries represented
- People native to the countries of study who would serve as primary sources for students to interview
- Art materials to make each country's flag and passport stamp
- Access to a video camera and video editing software

Sustaining This Project

Flickinger and Opel plan to expand this project as an interdisciplinary unit to introduce the curriculum to students in the fourth grade. As expected, basic information literacy, research, and technology skills would be taught in the fourth grade to ensure that the students, as fifth graders, are adequately prepared to efficiently work in groups. The educators also plan to purchase videos, books, and magazines to spread awareness of the various cultures represented at the school throughout the school year.

CHAPTER 3

Take-Home DVD: Improving Emergent Literacy Skills

T. K. Cassidy, Library Media Specialist
Betsy Thornton, Pre-Kindergarten Teacher

Dug Gap Elementary School

2032 Dug Gap Road
Dalton, Georgia 30720
(706) 226-3919
<www.whitfield.k12.ga.us/dge/>

Project Overview

Each high school in America is charged with reducing the student dropout rate. Ensuring students will graduate is a process that begins long before they enter high school. In fact, the library media specialist and pre-kindergarten teacher at Dug Gap Elementary in Georgia recognized that students need to be engaged in meaningful ways in their school beginning as early as possible.

Media specialist T. K. Cassidy and teacher Betsy Thornton realized that 75 percent of the school's kindergarten students did not have the emergent literacy skills necessary for future success. With several native languages spoken throughout the student population, these educators began to focus their efforts to meet the needs of these students and improve their students' opportunities for educational success.

Thornton and Cassidy developed a series of lessons throughout the school year that taught the pre-kindergarten students oral language development, print awareness, alphabetic knowledge, and phonological awareness.

While this instruction was typical and well intended, it was not enough to bring student skill levels up to grade level on its own, according to the teachers. So they took things one step further and created for each student a take-home DVD that students could use to practice their skills over the summer months. Using Boardmaker software <www.mayer-johnson.com>, the teachers created a series of posters that covered the letters of the alphabet and the numbers 1 through 20. At the end of the year, students went to the district television studio, where the educators documented their students' knowledge on film. The students read their chosen letters from a mini-poster of words and pictures beginning with their letters. Each child also created a poster representing the numbers, and they each counted to their number while being filmed using the artwork on the posters.

> **TIP**
>
> If you do not have enough children to represent all 26 letters of the alphabet, enlist the support of other teachers and staff in the building with whom young students would be familiar.

Students used the culminating DVD at home over the summer to practice their knowledge and to share their skills with their families, many of whom did not speak English as their primary language. Through their research, the teachers recognized that there is a direct link between parental involvement and student achievement. According to veteran sociology professor Joyce Epstein, whose research has helped educators develop more effective family and community partnerships, "Research shows that parent involvement improves student achievement. When parents are involved, children do better in school. Parental encouragement and assistance contribute to students' higher achievement, report card grades, better attitudes, and higher aspirations" (Shaughnessy; question 8). The teachers theorized that the simple fact that the students were the stars of their videos would encourage students and parents to watch the video together and cement an early educational relationship in the home.

Timeline

Teachers taught these skills over the course of the school year. Filming and production of the video were completed in several sessions over a two-week period.

Roles Defined

The Library Media Specialist Is Responsible For:

- Designing an academic DVD project for kindergarten readiness concept skills along with the teacher.
- Preparing the video equipment and organizing studio time for filming the students.
- Assisting the teacher throughout the year to support student learning of literacy skills.
- Coordinating the reproduction and distribution of the DVDs.

The Teacher(s) Is Responsible For:

- Designing an academic DVD project for kindergarten readiness concept skills along with the media specialist.
- Focusing nine months of instruction on the skills to be demonstrated in the DVDs.
- Supervising the creation of the posterboard cue cards to be used in the video.
- Organizing and recruiting additional adult helpers and volunteers for the final presentation.
- Communicating with families about the DVD and answering their questions concerning the project.
- Working with the media specialist to coordinate and prepare students for taping.

> Students used the culminating DVD at home over the summer to practice their knowledge and to share their skills with their families, many of whom did not speak English as their primary language. "Research shows that parent involvement improves student achievement. When parents are involved, children do better in school. Parental encouragement and assistance contribute to students' higher achievement, report card grades, better attitudes, and higher aspirations" (Shaughnessy; question 8).

Measuring Success

Anecdotal evidence: Do others involved in the project relate stories about student academic achievement that can be tied directly to watching the Take-Home DVD? Do students demonstrate new knowledge and understanding in kindergarten coursework? At Dug Gap Elementary, one kindergarten teacher said she noticed a significant improvement in the quality and quantity of the journal writing performed by the students who participated in the video project. Kindergarten teachers also commented on the amount of detail and explanations these students offered during whole-group discussion.

Testing evidence: How do students perform on kindergarten entrance exams or other kindergarten readiness assessment tools? Of a possible 51 points, the mean score of the students who participated in the Dug Gap Take-Home DVD was 36.3. This was higher than the mean score of all other students with pre-kindergarten experience, which was 32.97. For those without prior pre-kindergarten experience, the mean score was 11 (see Figure 3.1).

Participatory evidence: Are parents who were timid about joining in school activities more willing to interact at school? Are students more actively involved in school activities? Although long-term success is difficult to measure, kindergarten teachers noticed those students who were enrolled in the pre-kindergarten program at Dug Gap were more likely to be placed in the mid- and high-level reading groups.

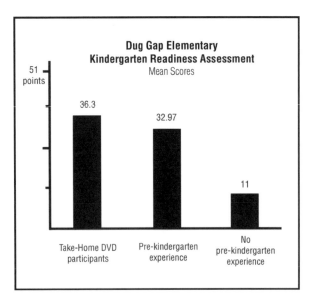

Figure 3.1: Kindergarten Readiness Assessment

Funding Your Project

Tap your district. Dug Gap received funding from the school district to purchase Boardmaker software. Because of the long-term benefit and the software's usefulness in a number of contexts, teachers could make a viable request.

> **GETTING SUPPORT**
> Tap your district's resources to purchase publishing software like Boardmaker.

Ask local agencies for assistance. Teachers utilized ink and printing supplies from the Georgia Department of Early Care and Learning, an agency with a direct interest in the *Take-Home DVD* project. Similar agencies exist in many states and can be found by going online to the state department of education Web site or by calling the education department directly.

> **GETTING SUPPORT**
> Get your community involved and ask for donations of ink and supplies from local printing businesses.

Materials and Resources

- Boardmaker or comparable software
- Posterboard cards to be used for the video that feature:
    - Letters
    - Numbers
    - Words
    - Other skills
- Video cameras and/or television studio setting
- Video editing and reproduction software
- Reproducible DVDs

Sustaining This Project

Thornton and Cassidy plan to introduce their idea to other grade levels. For example, they have considered developing take-home DVDs for:

- Reading practice of sight words for the kindergarten classes
- Math skills for first grade
- Grammar chants for second grade
- Multiplication skills for third grade
- Memorization of basic skills through music and movement for all grade levels.

The DVD easily meets the school's goal of creating opportunities to connect the home and school.

CHAPTER 4

Thinking Like a Scientist

Mary Karlovec, Second-Grade Teacher
Anne Michael, Library Media Specialist

Windsor Elementary School

264 Windsor Drive
Elyria, Ohio 44035
(440) 284-8014
<www.elyriaschools.org/windsor/>

Project Overview

Trying to help students perform well on state assessment tests when many do not have access to computers at home was a challenge for the library media specialist and a second-grade teacher at Windsor Elementary School. Working together, they decided to create a meaningful project that developed students' science and technology skills through creative projects and lessons that also involved parents.

The original idea was to develop a science and technology unit on inventors and simple machines. In the unit, they would teach second-grade students how to make PowerPoint presentations. Librarian Anne Michael first purchased grade-level-appropriate guided reading and big books materials, both fiction and nonfiction, to support all of the district, state, and national second-grade science concepts. She then developed lessons using technology that included sixth-grade buddies to help teach second-grade science skills. She put together a child-friendly Web page that included additional lessons and sites supportive of the science curriculum for extended activities outside the school.

> **TIP**
> Invite local experts in the various science fields to visit your classroom and talk to students. They may also be able to provide you with a behind-the-scenes field trip.

Michael aimed these extension activities to involve parents through home projects. Parents had access to the Web page and all library materials, and together they could show their child support while assisting him or her with individual science concepts. They also assisted the teachers with the evaluation process by participating in a "Show What You Know" night at the school.

But the teachers did not stop there. Students exceeded grade-level standards by learning to construct PowerPoint and interactive presentation board (SMART Board™) presentations in which they learned how to:

- Use a digital camera
- Develop graphic organizers for writing research projects using district-provided programs,
- Research using the Internet.

Together the teachers also developed science lab activities that used stimulating, standards-based low- and high-tech materials and reading and writing activities to support the science curriculum.

Timeline

This project was developed and taught over an entire school year. The collaborative team of teacher and librarian attended a variety of technology seminars as they were offered in order to get the technical skills and information they needed. They met weekly throughout the entire school year to develop projects for the science curriculum, to teach the skills, to train the older students, and to develop the various standards-based lessons.

Roles Defined

The Library Media Specialist Is Responsible For:

- Finding appropriate library materials to support science and technology skills and topics.
- Developing lessons for partnerships between grade levels to teach technology skills that support the science curriculum.
- Creating a Web page and making parents aware of and promoting the use of the resources for extension activities.

The Teacher(s) Is Responsible For:

- Defining science objectives to be met through collaborative effort.
- Working with teachers at other grade levels to tailor lessons that incorporate other students to meet those students' objectives.
- Making parents aware of and promoting activities they can attend and ways they can support the students at home.

Measuring Success

Anecdotal evidence: How did you know the new technology skills students were learning also helped them understand science concepts? Through surveys, the teachers assessed student experiences. Students answered questions such as, What specific activities were fun and meaningful to you? Ninety percent of the second-grade students thought doing the extension activities with the sixth-grade buddies helped them do better in science and in school in general. As an added bonus, 65 percent of the sixth graders thought the activities were good review. Overall, the second graders rated their experiences with the lessons in this project as 4 on a scale of 1 to 5. Parents reported that the activities were highly motivating and challenging for students. One parent who had students in two different second-grade classes said she saw significant differences in the knowledge bases of the two students despite the fact that they were being taught the same curriculum. She attributed the greater success to the innovative collaborative projects.

> "Ninety percent of the second-grade students thought doing the extension activities with the sixth-grade buddies helped them do better in science and in school in general."

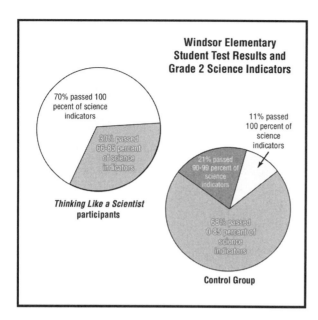

Figure 4.1: Student Test Results and Grade Two Science Indicators

Testing evidence: Does measurable student achievement indicate improvement on high-stakes exams? In the control group of students who did not participate in this project, only two of the students passed 100 percent of the grade-level indicators for science. Four students passed 90 percent to 99 percent of the indicators, and the remaining 13 students passed 85 percent or less of the indicators. In the class that participated in the project, 12 students passed 100 percent of the indicators. The remaining five students passed anywhere from 66 to 85 percent of the indicators (see Figure 4.1).

Participatory evidence: In addition to total student participation, how did the parents respond to their invitation to participate in the project? Ninety percent of the parents participated at the "Show What You Know" night at the end of the project. At that event, students demonstrated the extent of their participation in the project by reviewing all of the projects with their parents, a session that included two PowerPoint presentations and a gallery of students' photos. Students also reviewed with their parents a portfolio of three writing samples related to the weekly units, showing their parents the progress they had made.

Funding Your Project

Seek out available grants. Because of the emphasis on science and technology, the teachers were able to easily find a number of foundations and businesses offering grants for projects such as theirs. They funded their entire project with grants awarded to them by their school district, their PTA, and their local school district education foundation. They also received grants from Ohio Edison, Best Buy, and Hewlett Packard. To see an example of a school district education foundation, see <www.smef.org>.

GETTING SUPPORT

Utilize parents groups and grant writing to fund field trips.

Materials and Resources

- Computers
- Software for Web page development, PowerPoint, photo editing software, Kidspiration, CD-burning software
- Digital cameras
- Interactive presentation board
- Video cameras
- Library materials to support the curriculum
- Science lab materials

Sustaining This Project

To increase the length and the positive academic impact of this project, the teachers petitioned their administration to provide the staff with more collaborative time for planning and implementing units. The collaborative team worked closely together to determine how scheduling can allow more students to access materials, books, and extension activities. They are brainstorming ways they could offer computer nights in the school computer lab for students who do not have a computer at home. They are collaborating with the local public library to provide more convenient computer access for parents.

GETTING SUPPORT

Build support from your administration through evidence of your success.

SECTION II

Middle School Collaboration Units

CHAPTER 5

Where in the World Are Our Middle School Students Now?

Barbara Adair, Language Arts Eighth-Grade Teacher
Rick Norman, Language Arts Eighth-Grade Teacher
John Scrivano, Language Arts Eighth-Grade Teacher
Dana Thompson, Library Media Specialist

New Smyrna Beach Middle School

1200 South Myrtle Avenue
New Smyrna Beach, Florida 32168
(386) 424-2550
<http://schools.volusia.k12.fl.us/nsbmiddle/>

Project Overview

Graduating eighth-grade students at New Smyrna Beach Middle School in Florida finished the school year with many questions about Small Learning Communities. According to the New Smyrna Beach 2009–2010 *Freshman Registration Guide*, these communities are a "research-based, nationally accepted model" that "allows students to choose an area of interest and to be scheduled into their classes with students of like interests" (8). The intention is to simulate the real-world setting in which professionals daily interact, solve problems, and participate in higher level thinking with peers who share a common interest. Dana Thompson, the media specialist at New Smyrna Middle School, recognized that the eighth-grade students must be prepared so that when they enroll for high school they can make informed decisions about the Small Learning Community they wish to choose. Thompson gathered the support of the eighth-grade language arts teachers to collaboratively develop a career unit for eighth-grade students.

Working with the high school career connections coordinator and the high school alumni association, this collaborative team of teachers planned lessons and activities on career instruction and research, created a display that featured former students in their current careers, and scheduled career chats with area alumni of the school.

> **TIP**
>
> Make your alumni displays more relevant by comparing eighth-grade yearbook pictures with a current photo of the former student along with the career information about that graduate.

First, the eighth-grade teachers explained the career unit to the students, and each eighth grader completed a computer-based career inventory and assessment that Thompson purchased through a career-focused catalog. Using the information from the assessment, students selected a career and explored it through the use of various media, including the Internet, books, magazines, and interviews with people in that field of interest. The state of Florida required students to use FACTS.org, <www.FACTS.org>, as a research tool; Thompson also recommended students use sites such as O*Net OnLine, <http://online.onetcenter.org/>.

Working with the high school alumni association, Thompson found 40 area graduates who agreed to work with students at New Smyrna Beach Middle School. Thompson scheduled "Career Chats" over a five-day period to which students were invited if they were researching the various career fields represented. These sessions made these career fields more real for the students and were a meaningful way to involve the greater community.

> **TIP**
> Use this activity to increase your students' awareness of their community by inviting local alumni and parents to describe their careers. Emphasize the importance of education by encouraging students to research job requirements.

Students used their research and the career assessment to:

- Prepare for participation in the "Career Chats"
- Make an oral presentation using PowerPoint
- Write a final research paper about their career and their Small Learning Community choice.

By the time the unit was completed, students were armed with the necessary information—and the skill set—to research other careers if they changed their minds. The educators thought they had helped students move forward on the path to meaningful career exploration.

Timeline

This project had a lengthy timeline because of the complexity of the project. The collaborative team focused during the early months of the school year on creating the lesson plans, identifying resources, and contacting alumni. The unit itself took place over approximately six weeks in the early spring, prior to the registration period for high school. The staff felt that it was crucial that the teaching of this unit come immediately before the early spring registration period, when students had to select their small learning community for high school.

Roles Defined

The Library Media Specialist Is Responsible For:

- Identifying and gathering information about local high school alumni to be used in a display in the media center.
- Administering a computer-based career assessment.
- Instructing students in using various media sources to explore their careers of choice.
- Guiding students in creating PowerPoint presentations to share their career choices with classmates.

- Scheduling "Career Chats" for students to meet local alumni and discuss possible career fields.

The Teacher(s) Is Responsible For:

- Providing students with background information about careers and the education required to maintain them.
- Preparing lessons that teach students research, writing, and technology skills to be used when creating oral PowerPoint presentations about their career choices.
- Working with media specialist to collect information about alumni.

Measuring Success

Anecdotal evidence: *Do students talk with each other about their career choices? Is there still anxiety about signing up for high school classes once this unit has been completed?* Teachers overheard New Smyrna Beach students talking informatively about their experience signing up for the high school Small Learning Communities. Their conversations focused on the difficulty of deciding between career fields rather than expressing confusion and frustration about the general process. Teachers used these moments to start discussions with students about their career choices and future plans, which ultimately resulted in increased enthusiasm about their future possibilities.

Testing/standards evidence: *Referring to the specific standards met by this unit, do regular assessments lead to an improvement in student performance? Do research papers and student resumes indicate student understanding of their career choice?* This collaborative team constantly evaluated the career unit using a variety of methods to determine if it was meeting the requirements of the Sunshine State Standards in Florida.

- The computer-based career assessment and PowerPoint presentations fulfilled the standard of "learning essential technology skills." The presentation also met the standards of "using a systematic process for the collection, processing, and presentation of information" and "effectively applying listening and speaking strategies."
- Student research fulfilled the standard of using "media as a life skill that is integral to informed decision making."

- By writing a research paper, students "developed and demonstrated they could write an expository paper that is related to real-world tasks."

Participatory evidence: How many students are participating in the "Career Chats"? Has the word spread, encouraging more local alumni to be involved by sharing their career choices with current students? Local media covered the career fair and unit, focusing on the inclusion of local graduates as a "dose of real world." The high school alumni association willingly worked with New Smyrna Middle School to provide support and to encourage its high school graduates to stay in touch for future inclusion in the middle school initiative. All together, this was a very successful community effort that benefitted young people.

> "Local media covered the career fair and unit, focusing on the inclusion of local graduates as a "dose of real world.""

Funding Your Project

Look for local support. Ask local alumni business owners to provide publications or monetary support for materials that can be added to your media center as research tools for students. Be sure you have an accurate idea of the budget you will need. Try to put the funding together with a group of community contributors in order to spread the positive impact across the community.

Research grant opportunities. This team from New Smyrna Beach Middle School was able to purchase career software, career books, display boards, and other materials through a minigrant from the FUTURES Foundation for Volusia County Schools.

Materials and Resources

- Career assessment software (purchased through career-focused catalogs or online sites)
- Career books, magazines, newspapers, and selected Internet sites for research
- Display boards for "Career Chats" and displays in the library
- Digital cameras to take photos of former middle school students who participated in the unit
- Microsoft PowerPoint

Sustaining This Project

Whether or not your school utilizes the Small Learning Community model, all students can certainly benefit from career education. The topic is relevant to all students. Educators can design units and lessons on career education to meet many state and national education standards in addition to those identified in this chapter. Examine your school goals and test data; then plan a meaningful collaborative career exploration unit with other educators.

CHAPTER 6

Mathematical Nightmares

Nelle Cox, Language Arts Teacher
Shari Galgano, Technology/Math Specialist
JoAnn Reynolds, Library Media Specialist

Dover Air Base Middle School

3100 Hawthorne Drive
Dover, DE 19901
(302) 674-3284

Project Overview

What do you do when tests indicate your students are proficient overall, but glaring deficiencies in specific areas are evident when the scores are broken out into the specific elements being tested? This was the case at Dover Air Base Middle School, where 64 percent of students struggled in writing for an audience, but 95 percent of these same students scored proficient or better on the writing portion of the state standardized test. These students also showed above-average skills in the area of mathematics.

Trying to connect the dots and ensure that students show an equal proficiency in all of the elements of writing, media specialist Joann Reynolds and language arts teacher Nelle Cox collaborated with math teacher Shari Galgano to implement a cross-curricular unit that utilized student strengths to improve upon their weaknesses.

Using the theories of Dr. Ross Todd, a professor at the Rutgers University, and Grant Wiggins, an educational consultant on reform, the team created *Mathematical Nightmares*, a unit in which students were challenged to relate their mathematical prowess to an Internet audience. They closely aligned the unit to Delaware educational standards and benchmarks, and they developed rubrics to assess students' understanding of English, math, and technology concepts as presented in the unit (see Figure 6.1).

WEB PAGE RUBRIC

The following characteristics determine the success of the Web page in meeting the needs of the audience and fulfilling the writing purpose.

Score of 5	Score of 4	Score of 3	Score of 2	Score of 1	Evidence/Example
Score point 5 meets all the criteria listed in score point 4. In addition, a paper receiving this score shows an exceptional awareness of readers' concerns and needs. The student may have shown an exceptional use of: ■ Development strategies specific to the purpose for writing ■ Distinctive style, voice, tone ■ Literary devices ■ Compositional risks	Unified with smooth transitions, a clear and logical progression of ideas, and an effective introduction and closing. Sufficient, specific, and relevant details that are fully elaborated. Consistently complete sentences with appropriate variety in length and structure. A consistent style with precise and vivid word choice. Few, if any, errors in standard written English that do not interfere with understanding [of Web page].	Generally unified with some transitions, a clear progression of ideas, and an introduction and closing. Specific details but may be insufficient, irrelevant, or not fully elaborated. Generally complete sentences with sufficient variety in length and structure. Some style and generally precise word choice. Some errors in standard written English that rarely interfere with understanding.	Minimally unified and may lack transitions or an introduction or closing. Some specific details but may be insufficient, irrelevant, and/or not elaborated. Some sentence formation errors and a lack of sentence variety. Sometimes general and repetitive world choice. Several kinds of errors in standard written English that interfere with understanding.	Lacks unity. No or few specific details that are minimally elaborated. Frequent and severe sentence formation errors and/or a lack of sentence variety. Often general, repetitive, and/or confusing word choice. Frequent and severe errors in standard written English that interfere with understanding.	

Figure 6.1: Example of Web Page Rubric. Used with Permission from JoAnn Reynolds, Nelle Cox, and Shari Galgano.

Score of 5	Score of 4	Score of 3	Score of 2	Score of 1	Evidence/Example
All backgrounds, colors, font, diagrams, and graphics enhance the page.	All backgrounds, colors, font, diagrams, and graphics enhance the page.	Some backgrounds, colors, fonts, diagrams, and graphics are subtle and appropriate.	The pages appear "busy" or "dull." Text may be difficult to read. Some required components are somewhat unclear.	The pages are unattractive. Text is difficult to read. Required components are unclear.	
All links are consistent and easy to find so that the user can easily navigate back and forth through pages.	All links are consistent and easy to find so that the user can easily navigate back and forth through pages.	Some links are consistent and easy to find so that the user can easily navigate back and forth through pages.	The user may become confused when navigating between pages. Some links may not work.	The user may become lost, or links may be missing or not working.	
A complete and accurate bibliography contains links to at least 2 math resources and all graphics used.	A complete and accurate bibliography contains links to at least 2 math resources and all graphics used.	A complete and accurate bibliography contains links to 2 math resources and all graphics used.	Incomplete and inaccurate bibliography contains links to 1 math resource and all graphics. Dream sequence contains 2 math terms hyperlinked to the glossary and at least 1 external link.	No bibliography or dream sequence. Contains 1 math term hyperlinked to the glossary.	
Dream sequence contains at least 4 math terms relating to the story hyperlinked to the glossary of accurate definitions and at least 1 external link.	Dream sequence contains at least 4 math terms hyperlinked to the glossary and at least 1 external link.	Dream sequence contains 3 math terms hyperlinked to the glossary and at least 1 external link.			
Shows efficient and effective understanding of the grade-level mathematical concepts.	Shows efficient and effective understanding of the grade level mathematical concepts.	Shows effective understanding of the grade-level mathematical concepts.	Shows some understanding of the grade level mathematical concepts.	Shows very limited understanding of the grade-level mathematical concepts.	

Figure 6.1: (continued)

To get started, the students read *The Number Devil: A Mathematical Nightmare*, by Hans Magnus Enzensberger, Rotraut Susanne Berner, and Michael Henry Heim (Henry Holt, 2000). The story follows a young boy who has mathematical nightmares. As he sleeps, he is visited by the Number Devil, who helps him learn the math concepts that baffle him. Using the book as a model, students composed their own mathematical nightmare chapters. Students had to clearly communicate a mathematical theory. The students then developed their own Web pages on which they posted their stories. A sample of their work can be accessed at <www.teachers.cr.k12.de.us/~abmlibrary/NDstudent.htm>.

The unit utilized a team-teaching approach so that students could benefit from the knowledge of teachers in multiple, relevant disciplines at one time. This cross-curricular technique allowed the teachers to teach more skills in a concentrated time period and also showed students how to connect one subject area to another.

> **TIP**
> Convince your school administration to allow time during faculty meetings and in-service days for collaboration and planning.

Timeline

This is another long-term project. The project evolved over one school year. The team planned, implemented, assessed, and reflected on it the entire school year. The specific amounts of time spent in the various phases varied broadly.

Roles Defined

The Library Media Specialist Is Responsible For:

- Planning research lessons in coordination with the math and English teachers to teach students best practices.
- Coordinating the posting of student work on the project Web page.

The Teacher(s) Is Responsible For:

- Receiving parent permission for students to post work on a Web site (see Figure 6.2).

Dear Parents and Guardians,

Grade 8 is working on a unit that will incorporate skills taught in language arts, math, and library science. Your student should be able to tell you all about it! Go to the school Web site at http://www.k12.de.us/dafbms/ and click on the *Number Devil* activity. Books are available at school. To get more information about the book (or to order a personal copy for your child), check out amazon.com. The final project will be to create a Web site. In order to accomplish the goal, students will need an e-mail account. If they do not already have one, we can set one up with your permission. Please fill in the form below and have your student return it to Mrs. Cox.

It will be exciting to see students' hard work published on the Internet! Please discuss the project with your child over the course of the unit. If you have any questions, feel free to contact us.

Sincerely,

Mrs. Cox   Mrs. Reynolds

_____   _____

Nelle.cox@cr.k12.de.us   joann.reynolds@cr.k12.de.us

Please cut and detach

Student's name_____

E-mail address _____

If needed, you have my permission to set up a gaggle.net e-mail address for school use.

_____

parent/guardian signature   date

Figure 6.2: Example of Parent Permission Letter. Used with Permission.

- Identifying the areas of student weaknesses in math.
- Differentiating lessons to meet standards in math and English.
- Focusing lessons on writing techniques, specifically the creative writing process, to relate information.
- Teaching the interpretation of skills to extend the meaning of informative, literary, and technical texts to connect them to a mathematical schema.

Measuring Success

Anecdotal evidence: *Did students enjoy working with more than one teacher? Do you think they learned more by having more than one teacher involved?* At the end of this impressive unit, the staff polled Dover Air Base Middle School students, and the results showed that 53 percent of the students were glad that the math and English teacher were available to them to answer questions.

Testing evidence: *Do students' skills on state tests improve?* At the beginning of the year, an analysis of state test results showed that 72 percent of participating students demonstrated weaknesses in communicating math concepts in writing. Of these students, only 16 percent showed this weakness by the end of the school year, according to the state test results (see Figure 6.3).

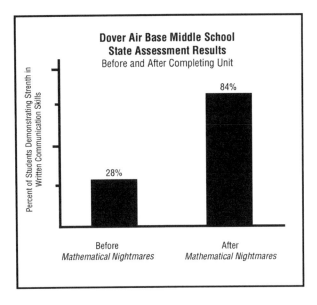

Figure 6.3: State Assessment Results. Used with Permission.

> Only 16 percent showed this weakness by the end of the school year, according to the state test results

Participatory evidence: *Are students excited to write about math? Do they work willingly, or is discipline a problem? Do students ask questions and otherwise indicate that they understand their assignment?* The teachers developed a survey that provided them with evidence of topical comprehension growth. They administered the survey to the students before, during, and after they completed the unit, which gave the team another tool to identify the students who were continuing to struggle with various concepts and skills. The survey also gave teachers immediate feedback as to what about the unit was working and what needed to be improved (see Figure 6.4).

Name_____

Answer the following questions concerning your project. Use the back if needed.

1. Write the title that best describes your research project at this time.

2. Take some time to think about your research topic. Write down all that you currently know about the topic.

3. What interests you about this topic?

4. How much do you know about this topic? Check the response that best matches how much you know.

❏ Nothing   ❏ Not Much   ❏ Some   ❏ Quite a Bit   ❏ A Great Deal

5. Write down what you think is *easy* about researching your topic.

6. Write down what you think is *difficult* about researching your topic.

7. Write down how you are *feeling* now about your project. Check only the boxes that apply to you.

	Confident		Excited
	Uncertain		Relieved
	Disappointed		Frustrated
	Satisfied		Confused
	Anxious		Other

Source: Adapted from Dr. Ross Todd's 23 Evidence-Based Strategies presentation.

Figure 6.4: Example of Knowledge Survey. Used with Permission.

> **The teachers also developed a survey that provided them with evidence of topical comprehension growth.**

Funding Your Project

Look for local support. The educators applied to MBNA Bank for funding to purchase novels that exemplified the type of writing the teachers would be teaching the students. They developed the list of books they knew they needed and then went out to the community to find funding.

GETTING SUPPORT

Find out if local businesses set aside funds for education-related projects that may tie into their business. For example, a bank might be interested because this project could help students learn how to explain key banking concepts to customers.

Materials and Resources

- Novels that give students examples of how written communication can be used to relay mathematical information, such as *The Number Devil: A Mathematical Nightmare,* by Hans Magnus Enzensberger, Rotraut Susanne Berner, and Michael Henry Heim (Henry Holt, 2000)
- Access to a Web server for the posting of student stories
- Other resources for researching specific mathematical concepts or additional information needed in the creation of student stories.

Sustaining This Project

Because students learned to make cross-curricular connections, this program could easily be modified to teach other curricular areas. To encourage further collaboration, the teachers made the entire unit available—including student work, handouts, timeline, and teacher tips—to others in the district and the state. They were invited to present at professional meetings of local English teachers and library media specialist groups in their school district and throughout the state. Their entire unit can be viewed at <www.teachers.cr.k12.de.us/~abmlibrary/NumberDev.htm>.

> **TIP**
> Share your best practices on the Web to give other teachers ideas about cross-curricular units. You might also post tips and examples of student work as a model for others to replicate.

CHAPTER 7

One Book, One School

Chris Altobello, Guidance Counselor
David Guest, Technology Teacher
Kendra Hamby, Assistant Principal
John McCollum, Principal
Debbie Pace, Reading 180 Teacher
Sharon Scott, Health Occupations Teacher
Brooks Spencer, Library Media Specialist
LaDonna Walker, Language Arts Teacher
Susan Wilson, Language Arts Teacher

Osceola Middle School

526 SE Tuscawilla Avenue
Ocala, Florida 34471
(352) 671-7100
<www.marion.k12.fl.us/schools/oms/>

Project Overview

Brooks Spencer had heard of one book-one school programs where everyone in a school reads one book at the same time, but she had experienced only single-grade-level reads. At Osceola Middle School, the library media specialist knew there was a need to help new students and incoming sixth-grade students make a smooth transition to the middle-school environment. She approached her district administration, school advisory council, and other staff members with an idea that she hoped would fill the need for community, renew everyone's love for reading, and get students involved in positive reading experiences.

Using the book *Red Kayak* by Priscilla Cummings (Dutton, 2004), Spencer and a group of teachers and administrators collaborated to develop a curriculum that met language arts standards and included plenty of cross-curricular activities. The book was selected because of its theme of doing the right thing even if it means losing friends. Spencer and her peers immediately saw its potential for reaching all students, grades six through eight.

The book tells the story of a teenage boy, Brady, whose friends drill holes in the bottom of a red kayak to vent their anger against the boat's owner. When this man's child, a toddler, drowns in a kayak accident brought about by this prank, Brady is torn between revealing who was responsible for the accident and protecting his friends.

Over the summer, Spencer and two other teachers on the team developed lessons, activities, and worksheets for the project. Spencer also made sure to order enough books, plus a few extra, for the entire student body and staff. They put together a study guide of the lessons, worksheets, and activities and presented it to the rest of the team. As a whole, the collaborative team worked together to implement the lessons so that all students would have the same experience while reading the book.

Beginning with the start of the school year, pre-reading activities provided students with a foundation of background knowledge. On the morning announcements, the principal or teacher reading the announcements gave students a trivia question for each grade level that was related to something they would need to know about before reading the book. Students entered their guesses, and a staff member selected winners from among those who submitted the correct answers. Because of the potential to win a prize, the students eagerly participated.

After a week of these activities, the principal read the first two chapters of the book on the morning announcements. Throughout the day, all of the language arts classes in grades six, seven, and eight discussed the first two chapters to make sure every student in the school understood what was happening in the book.

When the collaborative team planned this whole-school activity, they thought it wise to develop a timeline that allowed for different reading speeds while ultimately ensuring that all students would start and finish the book at the same time. To do this, the group identified a start, middle, and end point in the book. At the start of each of these predetermined periods, a staff member would again read a portion of the book aloud over the morning announcements.

At the end of this carefully orchestrated unit, a week of wrap-up and assessment activities kept the students' excitement level for the book at its peak. They willingly maintained their enthusiasm because they knew they would meet the author at the end of the week. Spencer arranged for a two-day visit with the book's author, Priscilla Cummings. The lengthy visit gave students motivation to actively participate in the learning activities based on the book and allowed them a more intimate meeting to ask their questions.

> "At the end of this carefully orchestrated unit, a week of wrap-up and assessment activities kept the students' excitement level for the book at its peak."

Although all teachers had a study guide of suggestions, activities, Web sites, questions, and character connections, the enthusiastic teachers in the school often came up with several other activities related to the book. Students participated in:

- Quiz games
- Scavenger hunts
- Words of the Week games.

Classes:
- Built a butterfly garden
- Filmed CPR videos
- Debated the legal implications of a prank gone bad.

The teachers' enthusiasm rubbed off on the students, who daily discussed the book with their peers as well as with students in the other grades. As media specialist Spencer suspected, the students and staff established a strong community across grade levels and age differences.

> **TIP**
> Do parents at your school have experience in areas that relate to the book selected for your project? Ask them to be guest speakers.

Chapter 7: One Book, One School

Timeline

A small group from the collaborative team met over the summer months to do some initial planning for lessons and key activities. The unit began with the start of school and ended in early November, covering a three-month period.

Roles Defined

The Library Media Specialist Is Responsible For:

- Selecting a book to be read by the entire school.

- Ordering copies of the book for each student and staff member.

- Ensuring that the library is equipped with the reference material necessary for planned activities.

- Creating a reference scavenger hunt and other library skill-related activities (see Figure 7.1).

- Working with the teachers and the school administrators to determine the appropriate "beginning," "middle," and "ending" points.

- Planning the author visit or other culminating event.

The Teacher(s) Is Responsible For:

- Developing curricular activities that meet standards for language arts and other curricular areas as appropriate.

- Compiling a study guide of suggestions, activities, Web sites, questions, and character connections.

- Creating or providing guidance for assessments of student learning.

REFERENCE REVIEW SCAVENGER HUNT
OSCEOLA MIDDLE SCHOOL 2007
B. SPENCER

Reference Sources to use:

Almanac—quick source of facts/printed yearly (use index and table of contents)

Atlas—maps/facts/location information

Dictionary—spelling/definition/pronouncement/part of speech

Encyclopedia—articles on a wide variety of topics

Magazine—published periodically - articles/facts/opinions/news

Newspaper—daily source of current events/local/state/world/human interest

Phone book—current listing or residents/businesses/government

Thesaurus—book of synonyms

Reference books—any book that will give you information on your topic

1. Locate a map of Maryland. List the four states that border Maryland. Near what body of water is Annapolis located?

2. State Facts about Maryland: What is the state sport? Who was the founder of the state? As one of the 13 original colonies, what was Maryland's rank? Where is the Mason-Dixon Line?

3. What is the average annual precipitation (rainfall) for the state of Maryland?

4. Where does author Priscilla Cummings live? List other books written by her (3).

Figure 7.1: Example of a Reference Scavenger Hunt. Used with Permission.

5. What is an "Eskimo roll"? (Hint: kayak term)

6. Which of the following butterflies would probably not be seen in Brady's Mom's Butterfly garden—Eastern Tiger Swallowtail, Delaware Skipper, or Mexican Silverspot?

7. Change the underlined word in each sentence to a more colorful word.

Sunrise over the Chesapeake Bay can be <u>nice</u>.

It was another <u>hot</u> day with no sign of rain.

8. What is a juvenile? When was this word first used?

9. What professional baseball team is located in Maryland? In what city does it play? What is the mascot?

10. Using the Maryland state magazine, find out when and where the Oyster Festival is held. (If the magazine is not available, you may use the computer.)

11. Using the newspaper, locate the weather section. What are the high and low temperatures in Maryland's capital city?

All reference sources, except the phone book, should be used. Some can be used more than once. Next to each answer, write which reference book you used, and be prepared to state why that was the one you chose.

Figure 7.1: (continued)

Measuring Success

Anecdotal evidence: *Is there interest in repeating this activity with other books?* At Osceola Middle School, the media specialist selected a second book and secured funds for an author visit before the school year was even completed. The faculty decided to start a young adult book group to discuss selections and select new titles for the club.

Testing evidence: *Do scores on assessments reflect student learning?* The school participates in the Accelerated Reader program. Staff used the program to administer the Accelerated Reader test to 884 students. The average score for these students, grades six through eight, was 90.2 percent. Other assessments included a critical-thinking "interactive test" in which students could use the book, each other, or other reference sources to answer questions in the form of opinions, citing sources that connected to the story (see Figure 7.2). Some of the teachers created a quiz game using computer software to test students' knowledge and understanding of the book.

Participatory evidence: *How do you keep students involved and interested?* One of the school's guidance counselors created a writing challenge. Students wrote about a guiding principle, such as respect, compassion, or courage, and how the principle related to the book. Winners received prizes for their entries (see Figure 7.3). Teachers in other curricular areas also became involved because the students' enthusiasm for the book was carried from class to class. These teachers helped students plant a butterfly garden and make a video about CPR, for example.

Gifted Classes   Name_____

THE *RED KAYAK* INTERACTIVE TEST

    This is an *interactive* test because you may interact with each other to find the answers, you may check out the book, your *Red Kayak* section, as well as the bulletin board, and you may even access the Internet. Please write your answers neatly on a separate piece of paper and on this test where lines have been provided. The test should be completed by the end of the week.

1. Draw a kayak and describe three ways it is *significantly* different from a canoe. (15 pts)

2. In your opinion, what is the climax of this story? *Support* your answer. (10 pts)

3. Explain the molting process of crabs and *cite your source* of information. (10 pts)

4. Explain the ABCs of CPR. (10 pts)

5. Fill in the missing effects and the missing cause: (15 pts)

CAUSE		EFFECT
Ben dies	→	Brady_____
	→	Mr. DiAngelo_____
_____	→	Brady's parents are apart and Brady has no closure.

Figure 7.2: Example of an Interactive Test. Used with Permission.

56

HERE IS A CHALLENGE!

Cite and explain a passage from *The Red Kayak* that demonstrates one of our guiding principles. You and three friends can win free movie passes and a scrumptious lunch at Red Lobster!!! Here is how it works.

Print the attachment and follow the directions.

Get three friends to participate with you. You can work together. They must have completed their entry form to attend the all expenses paid movie and lunch with you. Turn the forms in to Mrs. DeNaro or you may give it to your HR teacher to turn in to Mrs. DeNaro. If the information is filled out correctly, and you are the first to identify a guiding principle, what it means, and cite a passage in the book, and explain how a character demonstrated that guiding principle, your name will be entered into a drawing for the freebies. You must also state the page in the book where you found the example. Be sure you get the other three friends to submit an entry by identifiying a guiding principle illustrated in the book. The drawing will take place on November 5th when the author of *The Red Kayak* visits our school.

So start thinking about what you have read, get together with a few friends, skim the book, discuss examples you find where characters are demonstrating one of the 12 guiding principles, fill out the form and give it to Mrs. DeNaro. You may enter more then once but you must explain a different guiding principle. The more entries you have the better your chances become of winning.

Read, think, discus the book, and have fun. Try to make the 12 guiding principles part of your life. Your sure to be a winner and your friends will just adore you!

GOOD LUCK!!!

p.s. There might be a mystery guest of guests joining you and your friends for lunch at Red Lobster.

Mrs. DeNaro

Figure 7.3: Example of a Writing Challenge. Used with Permission.

THE 12 GUIDING PRINCIPLES

respect—to feel or show honor for; to think highly of to be thoughtful about; to have regard for

compassion—a feeling of being sorry for another's sufferings along with a desire to help

courage—the quality of being able to control one's fear and so to face danger, pain, or trouble willingly; bravery

responsibility—something one is supposed to look after or take care of; the condition of being responsible

initiative—the ability to get things started or done without needing to be told what to do; the first step in bringing something about

optimism—a bright and hopeful feeling about life, in which on expects things to turnout all right; a belief that there is more good than evil

honesty—the quality of being honest, truthful, and trustworthy; refusing to lie, cheat, or steal

loyalty—the condition of being faithful to one's family, duty, beliefs, etc; a steady devotion

adaptability—the ability to change so as to make fit; the ability to change oneself to meet new conditions

trustworthy—the quality of being reliable; deserving of trust

contemplation—careful and serious consideration; plan, expectation, intention

perseverance—continued, patient effort; persistence; the act of persevering

Figure 7.3: (continued)

Funding Your Project

Look at ways your school already raises money. This unit was partially funded with profits from the school's annual book fair. That might be a possible source of funding for many schools.

Talk to your education foundation and other education interest groups. The school advisory committee budgeted $2,000 for the project, which was used to purchase books. The faculty planning group for the project also submitted a request to the Public Education Foundation, which awarded the project $1,000. These funds made possible a two-day visit by the book's author, rather than a one-day visit.

> "A local business interested in what the school was doing donated $200 to the project. A local hotel gave the school a discount from for the author's stay. A local sporting goods store donated the use of a red kayak during the course of the project."

TIP
Look at fundraisers that already exist to see if funding could be used to help support your project.

Think local. A local business interested in what the school was doing donated $200 to the project. A local hotel gave the school a discount for the author's stay. A local sporting goods store donated the use of a red kayak during the course of the project. The kayak, central to the plot of the book, was placed on the school grounds, and teachers used it as a prop for various activities.

GETTING SUPPORT
Ask area businesses to contribute money or offer services to support your project. Pinpoint businesses that may have a connection with the topics in the book.

Materials and Resources

- An appropriate novel, such as *Red Kayak* by Priscilla Cummings (Dutton, 2004)
- Computers for research, including search databases
- Reference materials that support themes and situations in the book
- Copies of book for students
- Materials for additional activities related to the book, as planned by the faculty team

Sustaining This Project

At Osceola Middle School, the administration already encourages teachers to share ideas and extend them to other class lessons and activities. The library media specialist plans to expand work in other disciplines, like PE/Health, to see how quality young adult literature can bring understanding of heavy topics to the level of the students. Additional activities, such as a Battle of the Book competition, will encourage participation and interest throughout any future book-read unit. For more information on conducting a Battle of the Books competition, read *Motivating Readers in the Middle Grades,* by Joan Collins (Linworth Publishing, 2008).

> **TIP**
> Share resources with other schools in your district. If two or more schools do an all-school book read, these schools may be able to swap their books instead of purchasing new ones.

SECTION III

High School Collaboration Units

CHAPTER 8

Teen Expressions

Lorraine Grochowski, Library Media Specialist
Corrine Richardson, Reading Coach

Booker T. Washington Senior High School

1200 Northwest 6th Avenue
Miami, Florida 33136
(305) 324-8900
<http://btw.dadeschools.net/>

Project Overview

At Booker T. Washington Senior High School in Miami, Florida, all of the students in the intensive reading classes had below-grade level reading and writing skills. They struggled to pass the Florida Comprehensive Achievement Test (FCAT), and they showed no motivation to attend school regularly or do their best work from the time the test was administered in March through the end of the school year. They determined that, once they had taken the FCAT, there was no reason to make any effort for the remainder of the school year.

Teen Expressions was developed to increase the writing, reading, and research skills as well as to improve student motivation. Over nine weeks, media specialist Lorraine Grochowski and reading coach Corrine Richardson convinced these students not only that poetry was

> **Students built their self-esteem and confidence through these activities because they had a chance to express themselves during a challenging time in their lives as they became young adults.**

relevant to them but also that it was a tool they could use to communicate their fears, difficulties, and even joys.

The collaborative team first introduced them to poets, both historical and modern. They discussed with the students what the poets were trying to convey through their work. When the students began to show interest, the encouraged educators gave students assignments that allowed them to explore the types of poetry to which they found themselves making connections.

Students built their self-esteem and confidence through these activities because they had a chance to express themselves during a challenging time in their lives as they became young adults. They did this while conducting research about a self-selected poet and his or her works. They attended the library media center two times each week and researched their poet using FINDS, a Florida research model. Then they compiled this research into an expository paper about a favorite poem by this poet and a two- to three-page research paper about the poet.

The key to the unit, though, was the original poetry students created in a form of expression to which they really connected. Their original poetry centered on the theme of growing pains, which encouraged students to reflect on the difficult process of becoming a young adult. Each student wrote 6 to 10 poems. They used publishing programs, binding materials, and craft supplies such as decorative paper, markers, and stickers to create a book of their original poems.

The collaborating teachers gave these students the special attention and support they needed not only to open up about the emotional issues they were experiencing but also to do so in such a way that the students connected their education to their personal lives.

> **TIP**
> Have students compile their poems in a personal poetry book. Allow them to use various craft supplies, such as decorative paper, stickers, and markers, to make the books attractive as well as self-expressive.

These research and writing activities were preparing students for an end-of-the-year Poetry Slam. At this point, the students had invested their energy and emotion in their work and eagerly recited their poetry to an invited audience of students and family. Grochowski and Richardson assembled an anthology of the students' poetry and directed students to invite their family and loved ones to a very special Poetry Slam. The teachers reserved a special locale and arranged refreshments for the event.

Grochowski and Richardson also arranged for those who attended the Poetry Slam to receive a copy of the poetry anthology. With the assistance of adult and student judges, students received scores for the poetry they presented at the Poetry Slam. The judges then awarded students with prizes for the best poem, best poetry recital, and best poetry book.

To finish the unit, students wrote reflection papers about their experiences with poetry. The teachers were amazed by what the students revealed through their poetry. They opened up about peer pressures they experienced, relationships that hurt them, and their struggles with authority as they grew into their own independence. Although this unit was intended to teach students research and literacy skills, the students learned who they were and gained personal strength and self-confidence.

The district's Education Fund and supporting corporate sponsors recognized *Teen Expressions* as a successful, unique, student-centered project and agreed to fund the initiative because they recognized that it would help student achievement on the Florida Comprehensive Achievement Test. Better still, the unit provided students with the enthusiasm and initiative not only to become regular attendees during the final few weeks of school but to work hard throughout the entire school year.

Timeline

Grochowski and Richardson planned for the project to take nine weeks. Students utilized the library media center two times a week during the research component of the unit. Grochowski scheduled other classes so that they would not conflict with her goal of bringing the students

> "The unit provided students with the enthusiasm and initiative not only to become regular attendees during the final few weeks of school but to work hard throughout the entire school year."

to the media center each week. At times during the unit, the students remained in their classroom for instruction and independent learning, during which they would work on their various writing assignments. They returned to the media center during the latter part of their projects to use the computers in publishing their materials in preparation for the final activities.

Roles Defined

The Library Media Specialist Is Responsible For:

- Helping students identify resources to be used in researching their poet.
- Teaching students to use software to publish their original poems.
- Working with the teacher to organize and plan the Poetry Slam.
- Selecting a panel of judges for the Poetry Slam.

The Teacher(s) Is Responsible For:

- Assisting students as they select a poet for their research.
- Preparing lessons to educate students about the various styles of poetry and the poets who use them.
- Guiding students as they formulate their own poems.
- Working with the library media specialist to organize and plan the Poetry Slam.

Measuring Success

Anecdotal evidence: What are the students talking about when they are in class and working on their poems? Do their conversations reflect their learning? Two students at Booker T. Washington High School always seemed to resent being in the intensive reading class: they were disengaged and did not excel in their work even though the teachers suspected they were very intelligent. They complained that the poetry unit was boring and procrastinated about getting started on the initial project. To help pique their interest, the teachers showed DVDs of HBO's "Russell Simmons Presents Def Poetry" and had guest speakers recite poems. By the time they were creating their own poems and books, the students were hooked. One said on her book's dedication

> ❝ Students earned grades for their research and poetry analysis paper, their personal books, their committee group work, their performance at the Poetry Slam, and their end-of-year portfolio reflections. ❞

page that she even worked when her friends were out on a Friday night. The other, who was repeating the 10th grade, wrote several creative and touching poems, even reciting one at the Poetry Slam—and he was selected by the judges as one of the winners.

> **35 percent of these students improved their grades.**

Testing evidence: Are student scores improving on standardized tests? Do student poems and research papers demonstrate their understanding of the research process and poetry as a writing genre? Students earned grades for their research and poetry analysis paper, their personal books, their committee group work, their performance at the Poetry Slam, and their end-of-year portfolio reflections. During the Poetry Slam, a panel of adult judges used a rubric to score each student's performance.

TIP

Evaluate the students' work three ways. First, grade their research and poetry analysis papers, their group work, their performances at the Poetry Slam, and their poetry portfolios. Second, consider the rubric used by adult judges at the Poetry Slam to evaluate the student performances. Third, have students write a reflection paper about the project to show what they have learned.

Participatory evidence: Are students' attendance rates high and consistent in their reading classes? Are the attendance rates improving in other classes for these students? What is the turnout at the Poetry Slam event? None of the students who participated in the poetry project received a grade that was lower than the one they had received for the previous grading period. In fact, 35 percent of these students improved their grades. This was quite an accomplishment because before the poetry unit nearly 30 percent of the participating students had received grades lower than those they received during the previous grading period (see Figure 8.1).

> **When they looked at their attendance books, though, they saw they had a full classroom 92 percent of the time compared to 80 percent for the same period of time the previous year!**

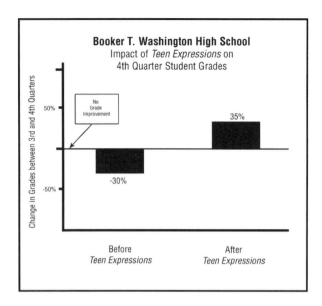

Figure 8.1: Impact of *Teen Expressions* on Fourth-Quarter Student Grades

Most important, classroom attendance during the final nine weeks of school improved greatly. The students' participation in the poetry unit was noticeable to the teachers. When they looked at their attendance books, though, they saw they had a full classroom 92 percent of the time, compared to 80 percent for the same period of time the previous year!

Funding Your Project

Look for local support. Ask local businesses to serve as sponsors of your Poetry Slam by providing refreshments free or at a discounted cost. Refreshments do not have to be elaborate. They can range from simple cookies and punch to a themed dessert buffet. This is also an opportunity to collaborate with the family and consumer science teachers and seek the possible participation of their students. Utilize school-business partnerships to pay for prizes at the Poetry Slam. This could be an opportunity to practice your minigrant-writing skills.

GETTING SUPPORT

Be creative when looking for funding for your poetry unit. Ask your alumni organization for assistance. Utilize profits from book fairs and other school discretionary funds. Check with your principal to see whether the project qualifies for special funding because it fulfills goals of the school improvement plan.

Materials and Resources

- Research materials about a variety of poets and their poems
- Examples of popular poetry, such as HBO's "Russell Simmons Presents Def Poetry"
- Computer publishing software, such as Microsoft Publisher
- Decorative paper, markers, stickers, and so forth for poetry book
- Prizes for Poetry Slam

Sustaining This Project

Finding an avenue to increase student motivation is important to any school's long-range plan. Use this project to help your school achieve educational goals in reading, writing, and research by targeting specific, discrete goals. Capitalize on the unit, and see that the personalization of poetry is an effective motivational tool for student participation and engagement. Keep students involved in meaningful units to improve attendance.

> **TIP**
> Encourage other staff in your school to get involved as a way to ensure the longevity of the poetry unit. For example, science teachers could have students write poems about science, and social studies teachers could focus their students on topics in history.

CHAPTER 9

Comic Relief: Using Graphic Novels with ESL Students

Leila "Bee" Manship, Media Coordinator
Chasity Markle, ELL Teacher

Concord High School

481 Burrage Road
Concord, North Carolina 28025
(704) 786-4161
<www.cabarrus.k12.nc.us/chs/>

Project Overview

Bee Manship, library media coordinator, and Chasity Markle, ELL teacher, noted that a significant number of the English Language Learners at Concord High School had not passed the state-required, standardized computer competency test. To make achievement even more difficult, these students demonstrated little interest in reading, going to the media center, or attending school, in general.

Deciding to collaborate on this issue, Manship and Markle applied for and received a Read2Succeed Grant to purchase graphic novels. These books would be the basis for a unit to inspire an interest in school while teaching a wide range of computer skills to equip these students for the North Carolina English I End-of-Course exam and the state's computer test, which covers word processing, spreadsheets, and computer ethics.

Utilizing Stephen Cary's book, *Going Graphic—Comics at Work in the Multilingual Classroom* (Heinemann, 2004), the teachers set goals to:

1. Teach the state Course of Study
2. Encourage critical thinking
3. Teach computer skills
4. Improve student attitudes toward books and reading while making students comfortable in the media center
5. Improve student listening, speaking, reading, and writing skills.

Using graphic novels, students engaged in and completed several activities, each building upon the previous activity. First, students responded to a picture from a graphic novel by writing a title for that picture. But titling the picture was not a simple task. The students discussed as a class the characters in the picture, the characteristics of these individuals, the setting, the colors of the artwork, and the action depicted in the picture. Students were required to speak in English.

After the initial conversation, students worked from the media center, where they were given basic instruction about operating the computers. Manship and Markle integrated computer terminology into their computer coursework. They recognized that, for the ELL students, this test was as much a test of their knowledge of English as a test of their computer skills.

The basic computer instruction led to the students' first assignment: to respond to a picture from a graphic novel and use the computer to creatively write out these responses using various fonts and styles, inserting pictures, aligning text, saving, and printing them. The educators continued to instruct students about the graphic novel form of writing. The students were divided into pairs according to personalities and English language abilities—higher level learners were assigned to work with struggling students so that they could help each other throughout the unit.

Meeting each week in the media center for three months, students gradually moved from writing their reactions to frames in the graphic novels to:

- Predicting outcomes
- Drawing additional frames for the novel being discussed
- Applying dialogue and color to their frames
- Studying the use of symbols, onomatopoeia, foreshadowing, and sequencing as they relate to graphic novels.

> **TIP**
> Involve your school's art teacher to help students perfect their drawings and to give students more confidence in their ability to accomplish their original artwork.

To complete the coursework, students used the Comic Creator at *Read, Write, Think*, <www.readwritethink.org/student_mat/student_material.asp?id=21>, a Web site sponsored by the National Council of Teachers of English/International Reading Association. During the last few weeks of the school year, Markle introduced them to Mexican American poet and author Gary Soto. She discussed with the students what was happening in Soto's poem "Orange," which is about a boy who takes a girl on a walk for the first time to a candy store. For two weeks, she taught her students about poetic devices, including imagery and characterizations. When the students demonstrated that they understood the poem, Markle divided them into groups to discuss how they would graphically illustrate the poem. They presented their comic strips as their final exam.

The teachers, working together, found ways to make school more inviting and more effective for one of the No Child Left Behind subgroups critical to the school's ability to make Adequate Yearly Progress (AYP).

Timeline

The unit began in early March and concluded with the final exam in June. During this time, students received instruction about graphic novels that incorporated English language and computer skills. The teachers planned the unit in February after receiving their grant.

Roles Defined

The Library Media Specialist Is Responsible For:
- Collecting and displaying graphic novels in the library media center.

- Coordinating media center time for the students to work on the computers and in groups to develop their comic strips.
- Working with the teacher to align computer competency skills with the content objectives of the unit.
- Tracking the circulation of graphic novels to determine the impact of the unit on the basis of the frequency and amount of graphic novels borrowed by students.
- Collaborating with the teacher to survey students about their attitudes regarding the project.

The Teacher(s) Is Responsible For:

- Identifying areas of the curriculum on which to focus lessons depending on the strengths and weaknesses of the students.
- Working with the library media specialist to select appropriate graphic novels for inclusion in various lessons.
- Teaching key English concepts and vocabulary to students in the ELL classroom and media center in collaboration with the library media specialist.
- Grouping students appropriately for project work.
- Developing a rubric to be used for grading the final comic strip and presentation.

Measuring Success

Anecdotal evidence: Do students talk about the graphic novels in their communication with each other? Are students conversing more freely in English? Do students express appreciation for the media center? The teachers surveyed their students and learned that Concord High School ELL students were interested in reading—but only after they completed the unit. At the beginning of the school year, Markle used a survey to assess students' attitudes about reading in general. They could check the various types of media they enjoyed or were willing to read, including books, magazines, comic books, graphic novels, newspapers, nonfiction books, and novels. Most of the students reported that they were not willing to read any of these items, while some students said they might read magazines and newspapers. A second survey was administered at the end of

> ❝ More than half of the students reported at that time that they liked to read and nearly all of the students said they would be willing to read graphic novels, comic books, magazines, and fiction materials. ❞

the year and included the same checklist. More than half of the students reported at that time that they liked to read, and nearly all of the students said they would be willing to read graphic novels, comic books, magazines, and fiction materials. Many of the students expounded upon their survey responses in the comments section, saying that they thought their time in the media center was the most interesting thing they had done during the school year.

> "Twelve of 13 ELL students and 74 percent of the English 1 students passed the end-of-course test in June."

Testing evidence: *Does student performance improve on the state-required tests in the areas of English proficiency and computer proficiency?* Twelve of 13 ELL students and 74 percent of the English 1 students passed the end-of-course test in June.

Participatory evidence: *Are students using the media center and its resources more frequently? Do students show greater participation in school activities?* At Concord High School, circulation data indicated a significant rise in the borrowing of graphic novels, from 7.4 percent of all monthly circulations in February to 12.1 percent in May (see Figure 9.1). Student absenteeism dropped, particularly on days when lessons were taught in the media center. When students were in class, they usually pleaded with Markle to work in the media center. Although most of these students had rarely visited the media center prior to the unit, more than half said on their end-of-year survey that they felt comfortable enough to visit on their own. Better still, students were more willing to read and remember literary elements, which certainly contributed to their test scores.

> "Student absenteeism dropped, particularly on days when lessons were taught in the media center."

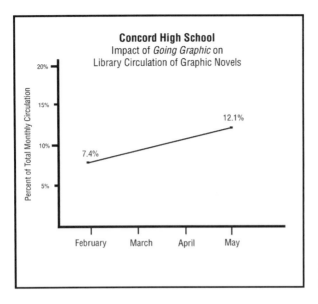

Figure 9.1: Circulation of Graphic Novels

Funding Your Project

Research grant opportunities. The teachers applied for and received a $1,000 Read2Succeed grant to purchase graphic novels for the unit.

TIP

Search online for organizations or businesses that offer grants for the purchase of books if your library budget is tight.

Materials and Resources

- Graphic novel collection for young adult readers
- Access to the Internet and multiple computer workstations
- Art supplies for the various drawing assignments
- *Getting Graphic* and *Getting Graphic! Comics for Kids,* both by Michele Gorman (Linworth Publishing)
- *Going Graphic—Comics at Work in the Multilingual Classroom,* by Stephen Cary (Heinemann, 2004)

Sustaining This Project

The teachers at Concord High School plan to provide focused weekly lessons through the school year that support English and computer curricula for the incoming ninth-grade students. They will also offer extended learning opportunities for students who demonstrate readiness to advance to the next skill level. These opportunities will introduce more English concepts, using graphic novels and the computer, and will be specifically targeted at the grade-level standards. Second-year English students will be required to have daily silent reading time and to keep a reading log.

To encourage more involvement from other English teachers at the school, media coordinator Bee Manship has provided freshmen English teachers with information about using graphic novels as a means to connect with struggling readers. Through one-on-one interactions, she is inviting these teachers to team-teach with her on a flexible basis.

To maintain the students' enthusiasm for the unit, teachers can hold an end-of-the-year celebration with ELL parents and present student comics in a book. If advanced students are ready, teachers can have them craft a final comic in which they develop and illustrate the entire story.

The unit had two components. First, students were educated about current Internet safety issues, including:

- Teen identity theft
- Potential damage to reputation
- Predatory or physical threats
- Dangers of "friending"
- Resources for more information and the reporting of problems on the sites.

For the second component of the unit, teachers required students to demonstrate their understanding of the lectures and discussions that the teachers collaborated to design. Using critical-thinking skills, students created an Internet safety brochure for middle school students. Esser and Knowles developed a rubric to assess the students and decided this rubric would actually help students as they created their brochures. They distributed a student version of the rubric to the students and explained that the components listed in it were to be included in their brochure. Using pictures, clip art, and other graphical elements provided online at teacher-approved Web sites, students creatively presented the information they had learned about Internet safety.

Knowles took her high school students and their brochures to the middle school, where they taught the younger students about the dangers and issues related to Internet social networks. Even at their age, the middle school students knew about social networking sites, and many had started exploring them. This early education had a dual purpose: to provide early education about Internet safety to the middle school students and to give high school students confidence in their knowledge of the dangers on the Internet.

> **TIP**
>
> Create a rubric with the various standards you aim for the students to understand. Distribute a user-friendly version for the students to use as a checklist for the elements of their brochure. By pinpointing the key standards, you will ensure that students are gaining the appropriate knowledge and developing new skills.

Timeline

Esser and Knowles taught the unit in six hour-long class periods. Students studied the information through videos and discussion during the first two to three days of the unit. The teachers gave students the remaining time to create the brochures.

Roles Defined

The Library Media Specialist Is Responsible For:

- Identifying and providing resources related to Internet safety.
- Collaborating with the health teacher to team-teach about these issues.
- Coordinating the use of computers to create brochures and the later distribution of the brochures to the middle school.

The Teacher(s) Is Responsible For:

- Providing class time for the unit.
- Team-teaching with the library media specialist.
- Creating a rubric for the brochure.

Measuring Success

Anecdotal evidence: Do students relate to the topic of Internet safety? Do students see how they may have misunderstood the dangers of the Internet? Teachers reported that students were very concerned about the personal information they had included on their social networking pages on sites like *MySpace.com* and *Facebook.com*. Many decided to make changes. Several students did not fully understand the difference between their physical friends and those "friends" who existed only in cyberspace. After discussing the difference, they made changes to their status on their networking sites.

Testing evidence: Can students demonstrate their understanding of Internet safety issues? Teachers assessed the students' understanding of the unit by reviewing the information the students presented in their brochures. Using a rubric, the teachers determined whether or not the students could accurately and concisely relay through their brochures the various aspects of Internet safety.

Participatory evidence: Are students who participate in the unit encouraged to apply their knowledge outside the class? Two students who completed the unit created a project on Internet safety for the Family, Career, and Community Leaders of America (FCCLA) organization and won the district competition, earning the right to

CHAPTER 11

Advanced Academic Literacies

Michaelyn Hein, English Teacher
Martha Hickson, Library Media Specialist
Mary Loder, Special Education Teacher
Caitlin Ryan, English Teacher
Lauren Sheldon, English Teacher

North Hunterdon High School

1445 Route 31
Annandale, New Jersey 08801
(908) 735-5191
<www.nhvweb.net/nhhs/>

Project Overview

Today's economy is no longer segmented by country or even continent. A collaborative team of English teachers, the special education teacher, and the media specialist at North Hunterdon High School developed a one-semester course, *Advanced Academic Literacies* (*AAL*), in recognition of the growing demand in today's workplace. There is a need for new employees with skills that expand upon the traditional reading, writing, and math to include awareness of global technologies as well as a strong understanding of science, economics, social, visual, and multicultural skills.

> **The administration, as well as the collaborative team that designed the course, felt that North Hunterdon students would be successful in the 21st-century workplace because of their participation in the class.**

She provided the classroom teachers with continual resource support throughout the research process.

The course became very popular among the students and stretched their abilities to achieve and understand the 21st-century skills the teachers intended for them to learn. The administration, as well as the collaborative team that designed the course, believed that North Hunterdon students would be successful in the 21st-century workplace because of their participation in the class.

Timeline

The idea for the course was developed by the English supervisor and an assistant principal at North Hunterdon. As a group, the team of teachers that designed the course began meeting in the second semester of the school year, before the course was to be implemented. They met once every three weeks and during professional days to work on general course content and the calendar of how the course would be implemented. Once they identified the curriculum content, the teachers worked in pairs to design each unit's lessons and materials. They reconvened and finalized their plans before the end of the school year. Team members who taught the class continued to meet twice a semester once the course was launched, and the entire group regularly communicated via e-mail to pose questions and share ideas.

Roles Defined

The Library Media Specialist Is Responsible For:

- Creating and teaching information literacy and other technology units.
- Team-teaching with classroom teachers when appropriate.
- Acting as a resource for students and teachers during the research process.
- Helping spread information about the course to incoming students, the faculty, and the community through newsletter articles and attendance at meetings with other staff and parents.

The Teacher(s) Is Responsible For:

- Creating hand-outs and other teaching materials for individual units within the course.
- Writing lesson plans to meet specific objectives and standards for individual units.
- Coordinating with the library media specialist to plan adequate research time in the media center.
- Helping spread information about the course to incoming students, the faculty, and the community through newsletter articles and attendance at meetings with other staff and parents.

Measuring Success

Anecdotal evidence: Do students recognize they are acquiring new and useful information? AAL teachers reported many revealing and helpful comments from students and staff. One student responded in a survey that the most important skill he had learned was to research efficiently. There are plans to start the course at the other district high school.

Testing evidence: How do students perform on assessments that test the knowledge they would acquire through this course? The Nelson-Denny Reading Test™ scores all improved by five percentage points by the end of the course. Students showed significant improvement in vocabulary, reading comprehension, and reading rates.

Participatory evidence: Do students show an increase or gain in the skills recognized as a need? Students' self-assessments indicated an increase in the percentage of students who were using and modeling responsible use of technology, from 86 percent pre-instruction to 91 percent post-instruction. The percentage of students who reported that they were able to design original work using desktop publications that communicated their learning jumped from 11 percent pre-instruction to 23 percent post-instruction. The proportion of students who used spreadsheets to analyze information, solve problems, and complete assignments went to 26 percent from 12 percent. Seventy percent of the students who had taken the *AAL* course could define an electronic database, whereas only 27 percent of the non-*AAL* graduates could do so. Only 45 percent of non-*AAL* graduates could spontaneously explain the

> **Students showed significant improvement in vocabulary, reading comprehension, and reading rates.**

CHAPTER 12

Culinary Reading Program

Wilhelmina DeNunzio, Director, Institute of Culinary Arts
Carol Faas, Library Media Specialist

Eastside High School

1201 Southeast 43rd Street
Gainesville, Florida 32641
(352) 955-6704
<www.sbac.edu/~ehs/index.htm>

Project Overview

The Institute of Culinary Arts at Eastside High School is one of the top-rated high school culinary arts programs in the United States, and each year students enrolled in the program are awarded thousands of dollars in scholarship money in recognition of their skills in the culinary arts. While these students are bright, creative, and motivated, a Florida state-required reading exam makes it difficult for several of these students to use their scholarships. Passing the test, which is administered from kindergarten through the 10th grade, is required to graduate. If a student does not pass either the reading or the math portion of the test, he or she has three additional opportunities during the junior and senior years to pass the test.

The culinary program is scheduled in such a way that those enrolled cannot take advantage of the reading courses offered at Eastside.

The Teacher(s) Is Responsible For:

- Developing lessons with the library media specialist.
- Providing content-area knowledge to help tie reading to the culinary arts.

The Reading Coach Is Responsible For:

- Administering regular testing to target student learning deficits.
- Identifying incoming students who will need additional reading assistance.

Measuring Success

Anecdotal evidence: Do students show enthusiasm for the lessons? At Eastside High School, students were eager to incorporate their new knowledge into their culinary program. They developed menus based on their topical research. They learned new techniques from famous chefs and used them in their food preparation. They learned how agricultural subsidies impact the price of food and the restaurant industry. They conducted knowledgeable discussions about how weather can also dictate the price of food. After researching and discussing the various social and political issues surrounding ethnic foods and consumption of locally grown foods, they developed an idea for a menu to use in their restaurant that featured Florida heritage cuisine. The school even received first place at a state competition—and the students who competed prepared food that was locally grown and locally unique.

Testing evidence: Do test results show a noticeable improvement as a result of the reading program? Fifty-eight percent of the juniors and seniors in the culinary program had passed the graduation test by the second quarter. By the spring, every student was eligible for a diploma. The average passing rate of students enrolled in the general program at Eastside High School is 50 percent. The educators are proud to say that the culinary program now graduates all of its students.

> **The school even received first place at a state competition—and the students who competed prepared food that was locally grown and locally unique.**

Participatory evidence: How can you ensure that all students are actively learning as a result of their participation in the reading program? The reading coach at

Eastside administered quarterly reading tests using the Scholastic Reading Inventory to identify any student weaknesses. Faas and DeNunzio immediate addressed the deficits and, when appropriate, involved parents and other teachers. As a team, they then developed a plan for the student in which all members of the team actively participated in helping the student to improve his or her reading skills. This might include additional homework activities or extra one-on-one attention in the student's other classes.

> "Fifty-eight percent of the juniors and seniors in the culinary program had passed the graduation test by the second quarter. By the spring, every student was eligible for a diploma."

Funding Your Project

No additional funding was needed because resources used in the project were already available at the school. If you do not have the resources available, this is a good project for which to seek local funding and/or resources from your local Chamber of Commerce, natural food stores and grocery chains, or farmer's market.

Materials and Resources

- Computer and Internet access
- Textual, visual, and electronic materials that support the main topic of the reading program (see Figure 12.1)

Works Cited

American Association of School Librarians. *Standards for the 21st Century Learner.* Chicago: American Library Association, 2007.

Buzzeo, Toni. *Collaborating to Meet Standards: Teacher/Librarian Partnerships for K-6.* 2nd ed. Columbus, OH: Linworth Publishing, 2007.

Eisenberg, Michael B. "It's All about Learning: Ensuring That Students Are Effective Users of Information on Standardized Tests." *Library Media Connection* 22: 6 (March 2004): 22–30. 21 Jan. 2009 <www.galeschools.com/pdf/Eisenberg.pdf>.

Lance, Keith Curry, Marcia J. Rodney, and Christine Hamilton-Pennell. "Executive Summary." *How School Librarians Help Kids Achieve Standards: The Second Colorado Study (2000).* 2009. Library Research Service. 21 Jan. 2009 <www.lrs.org/documents/lmcstudies/CO/execsumm.pdf>.

New Smyrna Beach High School. *Freshman Registration Guide 2009–2010.* Ed. Teresa Macks. 2009. Volusia County Schools. 23 April 2009 <http://schools.volusia.k12.fl.us/nsbhigh/Forms/9th%20%20Grade%20POS%20with%20Cover.pdf>.

SEDL. "The School-Family Connection: Looking at the Larger Picture." Ed. Chris Ferguson. 16 June 2008. The National Center for Family and Community Connections with Schools. 21 Jan. 2009 <www.sedl.org/connections/resources/sfclitrev.pdf>.

Shaughnessy, Michael F. "An Interview with Joyce Epstein: About Parental Involvement." 22 Nov. 2005. EdNews.org. 21 Jan. 2009 <www.ednews.org/articles/389/1/An-Interview-With-Joyce-Epstein-About-Parental-Involvement/Page1.html>.

Todd, Ross J. "The Evidence-Based Manifesto for School Librarians." 1 April 2008. *School Library Journal.* 21 Jan. 2009 <www.schoollibraryjournal.com/article/CA6545434.html>.

R

Read, Write, Think, 73
Reading circle, 98
Red Kayak, 50, 56, 57, 60
"Russell Simmons Presents Def Poetry," 66, 69

S

Scholastic Reading Inventory, 97
Self-assessment, 89, 90
Social network(s), 80; *Facebook.com*, 81; *MySpace.com*, 81. *See also* social networking
Social networking, 79, 80, 81. *See also* social network(s)
Soto, Gary, 73
Standards for the 21st Century Learner, 13, 86

T

Test score. *See* assessment
Todd, Dr. Ross J., 38
True Colors Personality Test, 86, 91

W

Warlick, David, 13
Wiggins, Grant, 38

Y

The Year of Eating Dangerously, 94

About the Editor

Kate Vande Brake is a newspaper journalist turned education public relations specialist turned editorial consultant. Although her career path has resembled a pebble skipping across water, her love of reading and writing has sailed with her. Vande Brake's inspirations come from the simple pleasures of life—bright colors, subtle humor, chocolate truffles—and she is often found teaching her two-year-old son the "important" things in life, like how to catch bugs and make mud pies. She enjoys taking spontaneous trips to large warehouse stores with her husband where they can sample prepared convenience foods and try, often unsuccessfully, to leave without a pallet of goods. Vande Brake's respect for educators has deepened as a result of the variety of projects in which she has participated over the years, and she is grateful to the teachers and administrators who helped prepare her for life as she knows it.